All-in-One Bible Fun

Favorite Bible Stories

Elementary

Also available from Abingdon Press

All-in-One Bible Fun

Favorite Bible Stories
Preschool

Stories of Jesus
Preschool

Stories of Jesus
Elementary

Fruit of the Spirit
Preschool

Fruit of the Spirit
Elementary

Heroes of the Bible
Preschool

Heroes of the Bible
Elementary

Writers/Editors: LeeDell Stickler, Daphna Flegal
Production Editors: Billie Brownell, Anna Raitt
Production and Design Manager: Marcia C'deBaca
Illustrator: Megan Jeffery
Cover photo: jupiterimages

All-in-One BIBLE FUN

Favorite Bible Stories
Elementary

ABINGDON PRESS
Nashville

All-in-One Bible Fun
Favorite Bible Stories
Elementary

ISBN 9781426707803

09 10 11 12 13 14 15 16 17 18 - 10 9 8 7 6 5 4 3 2 1

MANUFACTURED IN THE UNITED STATES OF AMERICA

All-in-One BIBLE FUN

Table of Contents

All-in-One BIBLE FUN Bible Units in *Favorite Bible Stories*

Use these suggestions if you choose to organize the lessons in short-term units.

Favorite Old Testament Stories

Bible Story	Bible Verse
Jacob's Ladder	Know that I am with you and will keep you wherever you go. Genesis 28:15
Joseph	My help comes from the LORD. Psalm 121:2
Ruth	May the LORD reward you for your deeds. Ruth 2:12
Hannah and Samuel	The LORD hears when I call to him. Psalm 4:3
Samuel Listens	I'm listening, LORD. What do you want me to do? 1 Samuel 3:9, CEV
David and Samuel	The LORD looks on the heart. 1 Samuel 16:7
David Plays the Harp	Praise God with trumpets and all kinds of harps. Psalm 150:3, CEV
David and Jonathan	A friend loves at all times. Proverbs 17:17

Stories Jesus Told

The Two Houses	You shall love the LORD your God with all your heart. Luke 10:27
The Sower	I treasure your word in my heart. Psalm 119:11
The Good Samaritan	You shall love your neighbor as yourself. Matthew 22:39
The Lost Sheep	The LORD is my shepherd, I shall not want. Psalm 23:1
The Forgiving Father	For you, O LORD, are good and forgiving. Psalm 86:5

All-in-One BIBLE FUN

Supplies

(This is a comprehensive list of all the supplies needed if you choose to do all the activities. It is your choice whether your group will do all the activities.)

- Bibles
- crayons, multi-cultural crayons
- balloons
- watercolor and permanent felt-tip markers
- pencils
- chenille sticks
- marbles
- construction paper, drawing paper
- large-size paper or newsprint
- scissors
- masking tape and clear tape
- modeling clay
- sponges, sponge shapes
- craft sticks
- shallow bowls or dishes
- tempera paint, paint brushes
- smocks
- resealable plastic bags
- newspaper
- white paper towels
- stapler, staples
- crepe paper streamers
- string, yarn, ribbon
- paper cups
- clear plastic glasses
- vinegar; corn syrup; lemon-lime soda; salt; onion; cookies
- white glue
- cotton balls
- cotton swabs
- large cardboard box, utility knife
- cookie sheets with sides
- sand
- plastic spoons
- paper clips
- index cards
- drinking straws
- lunch-size paper bags
- rubber bands
- 2 decks of playing cards, 2 boxes of toothpicks
- scarfs/blindfolds
- shoeboxes
- envelopes
- kitchen timer
- magnetic strips
- scarves or fabric squares
- biblical clothing
- dirt from various places
- clear plastic containers with lids
- paper plates
- dried lima beans
- magnifying glass
- spring clothespins
- trash can
- peat pots, potting soil, grass seed, flower seed
- feathers, felt and fabric scraps, wiggle eyes,
- ball
- mirrors
- sheet, blanket, or towels
- whistle
- scale, tape measure
- water
- CD player and CD of Christian music
- clean-up supplies
- handwashing supplies
- bow and arrow, fake fur fabric or towels, cane or staff, cooking pot
- grains of barley, oats, and wheat
- loaves of barley, oat, and wheat bread
- cutting board
- smooth rocks
- plastic tablecloth
- baskets

Welcome to *All-in-One Bible Fun*

Have fun learning favorite Bible stories. Each lesson in this teacher guide is filled with games and activities that will make learning fun for you and your children. With just a few added supplies, everything you need to teach is included in Abingdon's *All-in-One Bible Fun*. Each lesson has a box with a picture of a cookie,

We can listen to God's Word and follow it.

that is repeated over and over again throughout the lesson. The cookie box states the Bible message in words your children will understand.

Use the following tips to help make *All-in-One Bible Fun* a success!

balloon symbol

- Read through each lesson. Read the Bible passages.
- Memorize the Bible verse and the cookie box statement.
- Choose activities that fit your unique group of children and your time limitations. If time is limited, we recommend those activities noted in **boldface** on the chart page and by a *balloon* beside each activity.
- Practice telling the Bible story.
- Gather supplies you will use for the lesson.
- Learn the music included in each lesson. All the songs are written to familiar tunes.
- Arrange your room space to fit the lesson. Move tables and chairs so there is plenty of room for the children to move and to sit on the floor.
- Copy the Reproducible pages for the lesson.

Elementary

Each child in your class is a one-of-a-kind child of God. Each child has his or her own name, background, family situation, and set of experiences. It is important to remember and celebrate the uniqueness of each child. Yet these one-of-a-kind children of God have some common needs.

- All children need love.
- All children need a sense of self-worth.
- All children need to feel a sense of accomplishment.
- All children need to have a safe place to be and express their feelings.
- All children need to be surrounded by adults who love them.
- All children need to experience the love of God.

Younger elementary children (ages 6-10 years old) also have some common characteristics.

Their Bodies

- They are growing at different rates.
- They are energetic, restless, and have difficulty sitting still.
- They are developing fine motor skills.
- They want to participate rather than watch or listen.

Their Minds

- They are developing basic academic skills.
- They are eager to learn new things.
- They learn best by working imaginatively and creatively.
- They have little sense of time.
- They are concrete thinkers and cannot 0interpret symbols.
- They are developing an ability to reason and discuss.
- They like to have a part in planning their own activities.

Their Relationships

- They want to play with other children.
- They are sensitive to the feelings of others.
- They are shifting dependence from parents to teachers.
- They enjoy team activities but often dispute the rules.
- They imitate adults in attitudes and actions.

Their Hearts

- They are open to learning about God.
- They need caring adults who model Christian behaviors.
- They need to sing, move to, and say Bible verses.
- They need to hear simple Bible stories.
- They can talk with God easily if encouraged.
- They are asking questions about God.
- They can share food and money and make things for others.

Lesson 1

All-in-One BIBLE FUN ELEMENTARY

Jacob's Ladder

Bible Verse

Know that I am with you and will keep you wherever you go.

Genesis 28:15

Bible Story

Genesis 27–28

In the struggle between the two brothers, Jacob and Esau, Esau won the initial round in that he was born first. Jacob won the second and third rounds by tricking his brother out of his birthright and his father's blessing. Isaac's blessing meant more than a simple inheritance. A father's blessing promised the recipient good health, long life, prosperity, many descendants, and security. The power of his words was absolute, like a physical gift that could not be taken back once given. At the end the only blessing Isaac could give his eldest son was one of bitterness and struggle.

Jacob did experience some setbacks, however. What good was a father's blessing if the recipient son couldn't live in the land on which the promise was to be fulfilled? But God had a plan for Jacob and even used his character flaws to fulfill this plan.

Ultimately the covenant was continued through Jacob, not Esau, the firstborn. How reassuring to know that God forgave Jacob, supported him in his despair, armed him with confidence, and continued to use him to fulfill God's promise.

Television, comic books, fairy tales, computer games, and stories for children celebrate the wiley hero or heroine who achieves a successful end through deception. Children quickly learn that they too can use their skills to get what they want. When they hear today's story, they may be more intrigued by Jacob's plot than they are upset by the means he used to accomplish his end. He achieved his goal, but he had to leave everything he loved as a consequence. Help the children see that even though Jacob did something thoroughly despicable, God still saw something good in him. God forgave Jacob and gave him a chance to redeem himself. God is always with us, even when we aren't the most lovable of people.

God's love is always with me.

If time is limited, we recommend those activities that are noted in **boldface**. Depending on your time and the number of children, you may be able to include more activities.

Activity	Time	Supplies	
Hands Only Game	**10 minutes**	**paper lunch bags; rubber bands; paper cups; large piece of paper; markers, marbles, modeling clay, balloons (not inflated), sponge shapes, stuffed lamb, or other items available in your classroom**	Join the Fun
Finger Reading	5 minutes	Reproducible 1B (bottom), white glue, messages	Join the Fun
Sniff It Out!	5 minutes	five clear plastic glasses, vinegar, corn syrup, water, lemon-lime soda, salt, spoon, two paper bags, onion cut in half, cookies	Bible Story Fun
Sing the Story	5 minutes	None	Bible Story Fun
Bible Story: The Stairway to Heaven	**10 minutes**	**blanket, bow and arrow, fake fur fabric or towels, cane or staff, cooking pot, spoon, biblical clothing**	Bible Story Fun
Walking Angels	10 minutes	Reproducible 1A, business-sized envelopes, white glue, crayons or felt-tip markers, magnetic strips, scissors, construction paper or craft sticks, cotton balls	Bible Story Fun
Rock Tag	10 minutes	construction paper, scissors, masking tape	Live the Fun
Hop the Ladder	**5 minutes**	**Reproducible 1B, scissors, masking tape**	Live the Fun

Hands Only Game

Supplies

paper lunch bags; rubber bands; paper cups; large piece of paper; markers, marbles, modeling clay, balloons (not inflated), sponge shapes, stuffed lamb, or other items available in your classroom

Before the children arrive, place a paper cup inside each lunch bag. Inside the paper cup place one of the items listed. (You may add items of your own.) Put a rubber band around the top of each sack so that the children cannot see inside the bag. Write a letter or number on the outside of the bag. Set the bags around the room.

Create a grid on the wall with a box for each bag. As the children move about the room, they will write on the grid what they think is in the bag. (If you have non-readers, have a teacher stand at the grid and write the child's suggestions.)

As the children arrive, greet them warmly and get them started.

Say: Go around the room and try to discover what is in each bag. The only catch is that all you can do is feel it. When you think you know, go over to the chart and record your guess.

When everyone has had a chance to feel the insides of the bag, go over the chart. Then take the contents out and show it to the children.

Say: In today's Bible story a young man is able to fool his father because his father is blind. But even though what he does is wrong, he soon discovers an important fact:

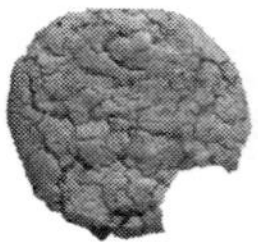

God's love is always with me.

Finger Reading

Supplies

Reproducible 1B (bottom), white glue, messages

Before class make a copy of the Braille alphabet **(Reproducible 1B, bottom)**. Cut the alphabet grid and the Braille message apart from the ladder words. Put a drop of white glue on each of the darkened circles. Allow the glue to dry. If you have a large class, make several as a timesaver. The message is: God's love is always with me.

Say: Some people who cannot see well use a special alphabet called Braille. They read the alphabet with their fingers. I have prepared a message for you to "read with your fingers."

Let the children feel the message: God's love is always with me. If you have time, let the children write their names using Braille grids that they create. You may prepare several blank ones for the children to use.

Sniff It Out!

Supplies

five clear plastic glasses; vinegar, corn syrup, water, lemon-lime soda, salt; spoon, two paper bags, onion cut in half, cookies

Before class, set the five glasses on a table. In one glass pour white vinegar. In one glass pour clear corn syrup. In one glass pour water. In one glass pour water and stir in two tablespoons of salt. In the last glass pour lemon-lime soda. Put the onion in one paper bag and the cookies in the second bag. Fold over the tops of the bags. Gather the children around the table.

Say: Here are five glasses. Two of these glasses hold something to drink. Three of the glasses hold something you could drink, but two of them I wouldn't want to. The puzzle is for you to figure out what each one is without tasting them.

Ask: How would you do it? *(Smell the various glasses.)* **Why couldn't you just look at the glasses and tell?** *(They look alike.)* *(Hold up the two bags.)* **Who is going to choose what we have for a snack today? Do you trust him or her to decide?**

Select one child to make the decision. Encourage the child to use his or her sense of smell.

Sing the Story

Supplies

None

Sing together the song "The Two Sons" to the tune of "She'll Be Coming 'Round the Mountain."

The Two Sons
(Tune: "She'll Be Coming 'Round the Mountain")

O-o Isaac and Rebekah had two sons.
O-o Isaac and Rebekah had two sons.
O the first son was named Esau,
and the second was named Jacob,
O-o Isaac and Rebekah had two sons.

O-o Jacob and his brother had a fight.
O-o Jacob and his brother had a fight.
'Cause Jacob tricked his father and he took his brother's blessing.
O-o Jacob and his brother had a fight.

O-o Jacob had to run away and hide.
O-o Jacob had to run away and hide.
He left Isaac and Rebekah and then ran to Uncle Laban.
O-o Jacob had to run away and hide.

O-o Jacob had to stop so he could sleep.
O-o Jacob had to stop so he could sleep.
Now a rock became his pillow as he closed his eyes in slumber.
O-o Jacob had to stop so he could sleep.

O-o Jacob had a dream and heard God speak.
O-o Jacob had a dream and heard God speak.
He saw angels climb a ladder and he knew that God was with him.
O-o Jacob had a dream and heard God speak.

The Stairway to Heaven

by LeeDell Stickler

Invite the children to participate in a pantomime. A narrator will read the story aloud while the children do the actions of the story. Stage directions are suggested.

Characters: Isaac—a blind, infirm old man; Rebekah—Isaac's wife, middle-aged, shrewd, and cunning; Esau—a young man, the outdoors type; Jacob—a wiley young man

Props for the story: blanket for Isaac, bow and arrow for Esau, fake fur fabric or towels, cane or staff, cooking pot, spoon for Jacob, biblical clothing

Isaac was very old. Before he died, he wanted to bestow the blessing of the older son on his son Esau. *(Isaac teeters in and lies down on his pallet. Isaac has a cane.)*

"Esau, Esau!" Isaac called out. "Come here." *(Esau scurries in and kneels at his father's bedside.)*

"Esau, I would like to taste that stew you make just one more time before I die. Then I will give you the blessing of the oldest son."

Esau was very happy. *(Esau jumps up and down; picks up the bow and arrow, then exits.)* He picked up his bow and arrow and headed out to hunt for the meat for the stew. Esau laughed to himself. Jacob may have stolen his birthright, but Jacob would not steal his blessing.

Rebekah overheard what Isaac said to Esau. She loved Esau, but she loved Jacob even better. So she called Jacob to her. *(Jacob comes running to his mother.)*

"Hurry, Jacob," said his mother. "I will make a delicious stew for you take it to your father. *(Rebekah sets out the cooking pot.)* You will pretend that you are Esau. Your father will bless you instead."

"But Mother, Father may be blind, but he is not stupid. He will know the difference. Esau's skin is hairy; mine is smooth. Esau smells of the field and the hunt," said Jacob, wrinkling up his nose. "I don't."

Rebekah rubbed her chin as she thought. "We'll cover your back and arms with dried goat skin.

You'll feel hairy like Esau. You'll even smell like him." *(Rebekah stirs the pot. Jacob dresses in fake fur or a towel.)*

When the stew was ready, Jacob carried it to his father. *(Jacob takes the cooking pot to Isaac.)* "Here's your dinner, Father. I'm ready now for my blessing."

"Esau? You don't sound like yourself. You sound more like Jacob," said Isaac, holding his hand to his ear. "Come here and let me touch you." Isaac reached for Jacob. *(Jacob kneels beside Isaac.)* Isaac ran his hand over the goat skin.

"Let me smell you." said Isaac as he sniffed his son. "Well, you sound like Jacob, but you feel and smell like Esau. Here, let me bless you." Isaac laid his hands on Jacob's head.

(Esau enters.) Then Esau returned from hunting. When he discovered what his brother had done, he was very angry.

"He did it again! He did it again!" Esau shouted and grabbed for his bow. *(Esau chases after Jacob.)*

Rebekah called Jacob to come to her. *(Jacob goes to Rebekah.)* "You must go to your Uncle Laban. Stay there until Esau's anger cools. I will send for you." *(Rebekah exits.)*

(Jacob walks in place.) So Jacob set off on his journey. He was a little sad. What good was a birthright and a blessing if he could not live in the land where it would be fulfilled? But he knew his life was in danger.

When night came, Jacob was so tired he could not walk another step. *(Jacob stops.)* So Jacob spread his coat on the ground as a bed. He used a stone for a pillow and went to sleep. *(Jacob lies down.)*

Jacob dreamed. In his dream he saw a stairway that stretched from earth to heaven. Going up and down this stairway were angels. At the top of the stairway Jacob could hear the voice of God. "Jacob, I am with you and will keep you wherever you go."

(Jacob sits up.) When Jacob woke up, he took the rock he had used as a pillow and set it as a reminder of God's promise. Jacob knew then that even though he had done wrong, God still loved him and would bring him home again.

Supplies

Reproducible 1A, business-sized envelopes, white glue, crayons or felt-tip markers, magnetic strips, scissors, construction paper or craft sticks; cotton balls

Walking Angels

Say: In today's story we heard about a stairway that went from the earth to heaven. Going up and down that stairway were angels. Let's make this stairway to remind us that God is not far away. God is right here with us on earth. No matter where we go or what we do, God's love is always there.

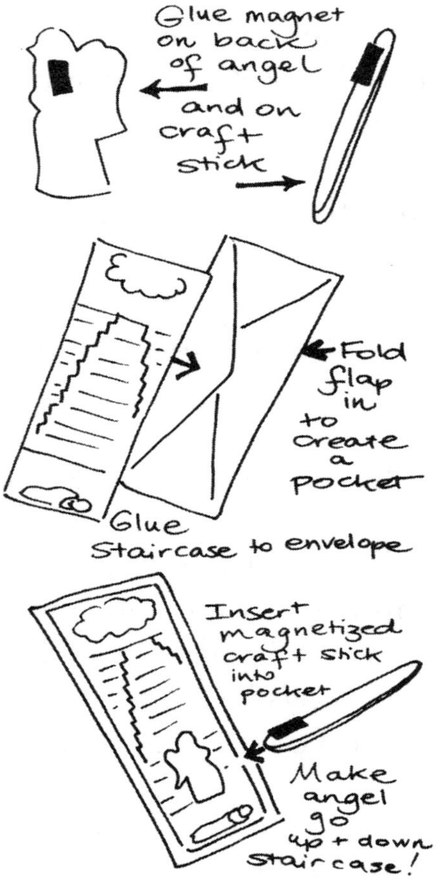
Glue magnet on back of angel
and on craft stick
Fold flap in to create a pocket
Glue Staircase to envelope
Insert magnetized craft stick into pocket
Make angel go up + down staircase!

Photocopy the stairway and the angel **(Reproducible 1A)** for each child. Have the children cut out the stairway along the solid line of the rectangle. Then have the children cut out the angel.

Have the children tuck the flap of the envelope inside itself. Glue the stairway onto the front of the envelope. Glue cotton balls at the top to represent heaven.

Have the children color their stairways and angels.

Cut one-half inch lengths from the magnetic strips, two for each child. Have the children glue one magnet to the back of the angels as shown in the illustration.

Give each child half a piece of construction paper. Have the child fold the construction paper over and over, forming an inch-wide paper stick. (You may substitute a wooden craft stick.) Instruct the children to glue the second magnetic strip piece to the top of the stick.

Show the children how to slip the paper stick into the envelope from the side. Help the children hold the angel until the magnet on the stick catches the angel.

Encourage the children to move the angel up and down the stairway.

God's love is always with me.

Rock Tag

Supplies

construction paper, scissors, masking tape

Cut pieces of construction paper into irregular shapes to resemble rocks. Make sure there is one rock for each child, minus one. Scatter the rocks about the room. Secure the rocks to the floor with a loop of masking tape.

Say: In today's Bible story Jacob used a rock for a pillow. After his dream he took this rock, stood it up, and poured oil over it. Jacob knew that he had done wrong. But the rock reminded Jacob that God still cared about him and would bring him safely back to his homeland again.

Say: Let's play a game. In our game the only safe places in the room are the rocks. A child who is moving between rocks can be tagged. A child who is standing on a rock is safe.

Select one child to be "IT." If IT tags a child who is moving between rocks, then the two exchange places. No one can stand on a rock for more than ten seconds (a slow count to ten). Two children may not occupy the same rock. If a person comes to a rock, then the person who was there must leave.

Play the game until several children have an opportunity to be IT. Remind the children that the rock reminded Jacob that God's love is always with him.

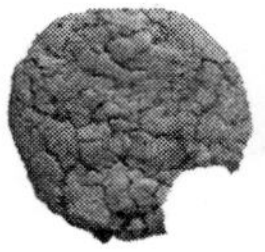

God's love is always with me.

Hop the Ladder

Supplies

Reproducible 1B, scissors, masking tape

Photocopy and cut apart the Bible verse words **(Reproducible 1B)**. Create a ladder on the floor using strips of masking tape. Make two sides about ten feet long and nine crossbars, with about one foot of space between each one. This will create eight spaces. Tape one of the Bible verse words in the space between each rung of the ladder.

Say: Jacob did something he should not have done. He cheated his brother. He deceived his father. But he learned an important lesson. God would be with him, no matter where he went.

Have the children hop the ladder, saying the Bible verse as they work their way to the top. Give each person a hug at the top. When everyone has hopped the ladder, have the children form a friendship circle.

Pray: Dear God, we are so glad that you will love us, no matter what we do. We are so glad that you are with us wherever we go. Amen.

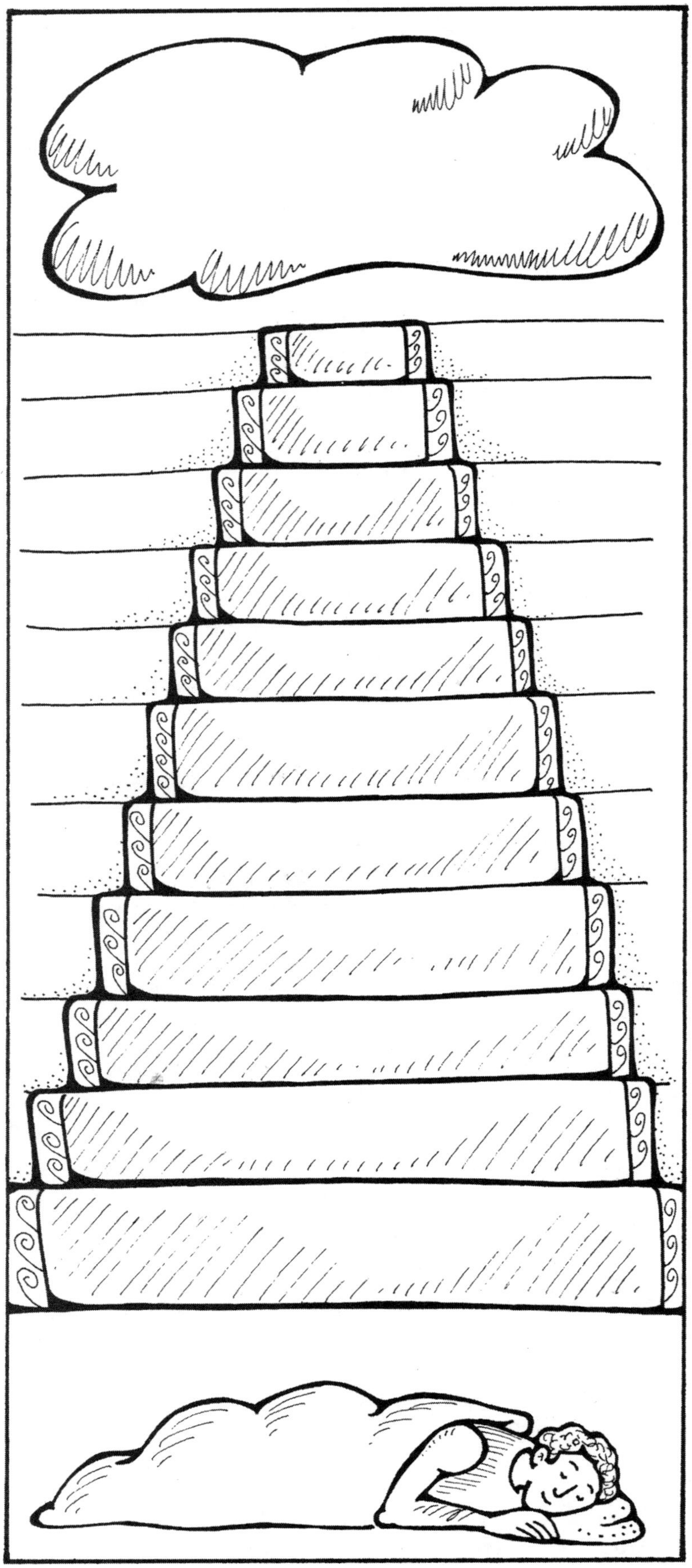

REPRODUCIBLE 1A

Know	that
I am	with you
and will	keep you
you go.	wherever

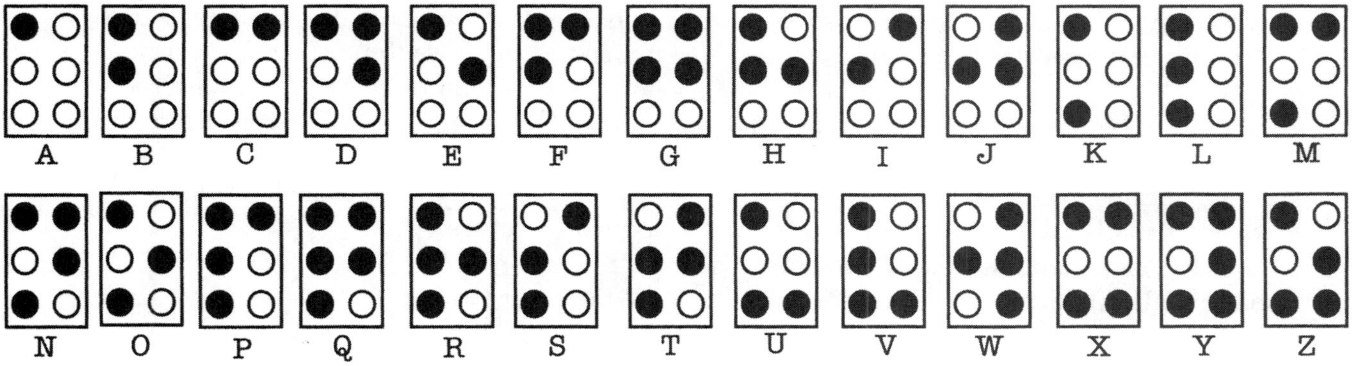

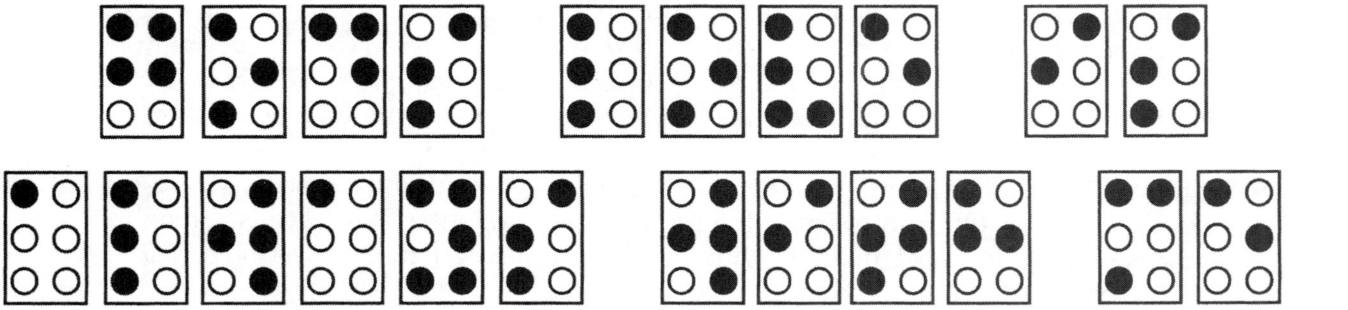

Reproducible 1B

Joseph

Bible Verse

My help comes from the LORD.

Psalm 121:2

Bible Story

Genesis 37

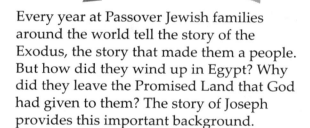

Every year at Passover Jewish families around the world tell the story of the Exodus, the story that made them a people. But how did they wind up in Egypt? Why did they leave the Promised Land that God had given to them? The story of Joseph provides this important background.

Jacob, after his many adventures, was led by God back to Canaan, where he and his family became even more prosperous. Jacob, however, made the same tactical error that his father Isaac had made by not treating his sons equally. Because Rachel was Jacob's favorite wife, Jacob naturally showered more of his affection on her sons, Joseph and Benjamin. This favoritism created jealous feelings among the other siblings.

One gift in particular created a problem for Joseph, the next-to-the-youngest son. The Scriptures say Jacob gave Joseph a coat with long flowing sleeves, totally impractical for anyone working outdoors, particularly with sheep. The coat constantly reminded Joseph's brothers of their father's special love for Joseph.

Joseph's dreams also annoyed his brothers. Not only did God talk to Joseph through these dreams, but God also made it clear that some day Joseph would rule over his family. This did not go over well with the family. However, this God-given ability to interpret dreams was eventually responsible for Joseph's rise through the Egyptian power structure.

At the beginning of story we find Joseph on his way to Egypt. By the end of the story Joseph is a man of great power and responsibility. How did all these changes take place? Joseph is a wonderful example of God's plans being fulfilled. God was there, and God continued to work through Joseph in every situation. Because of Joseph's gift thousands of people were kept from starving. All of his travails had only served to prepare him for the job he had to do.

God has a special plan for each of us.

If time is limited, we recommend those activities that are noted in **boldface**. Depending on your time and the number of children, you may be able to include more activities.

Activity	Time	Supplies
Join the Fun		
Rainbow Robes	**10 minutes**	**Reproducible 2A, cotton swabs, newspaper, small bowls, water, food coloring, scissors, plain white paper towels, smocks**
Jealousy	10 minutes	Reproducible 2B, scissors, envelopes
Bible Story Fun		
Clothespin Tag	10 minutes	spring clothespins, chairs, blankets or sheets
Sing the Story	5 minutes	None
Bible Story: Joseph, Man of the Year	**10 minutes**	**None**
Parrot Talk	5 minutes	None
Pharaoh Says	5 minutes	None
Live the Fun		
Turn About Tales	5 minutes	None
Prayer Signs	**5 minutes**	**None**

Supplies

Reproducible 2A, cotton swabs, newspaper, small bowls, water, food coloring, scissors, plain white paper towels, smocks

Rainbow Robes

Make a copy of Joseph's coat **(Reproducible 2A)**. Cut out the pattern. Using the pattern, cut one coat for each child from a plain, white paper towel. Cover the work surfaces with newspaper. Set small bowls of food coloring and water on the tables.

Greet the children as they arrive. Direct each child to a table where the supplies have been set out. Have the children wear smocks.

Say: Today's Bible story is about a brother who was not particularly likable. One of the things that made his family dislike him so much was a special coat his father had given him. Use the food coloring and water to decorate your special coat.

When the children finish with their coats, set them aside to dry.

Supplies

Reproducible 2B, scissors, envelopes

Jealousy

Photocopy and cut apart the trade items **(Reproducible 2B)**. Put one in each envelope. If you have more than eight children in class, make two copies of the items. Leave out the second "GOTCHA" card. Spread the envelopes out on a table. Bring the children together in a circle.

Ask: Has a friend or family member ever gotten something really special? Did you ever wish you had gotten something like it, or even better?

Say: Let's play a game. The object of the game is to get the most important prize without getting the GOTCHA card. Each of you will have a choice, except for the first person. You either can get your own envelope or can trade with someone else who has already gotten a prize. Do you want what your neighbor's got, or are you willing to take a chance?

Choose a child to be first. Have the children number off beginning with "1." Have the number 1 child choose an envelope. When he or she opens the envelope, have him or her hold up the picture. Everyone will cheer.

Ask the child who is number 2: ***(Name)*, do you want what number 1 has, or do you want to take a chance on getting something better?**

Play until someone gets the GOTCHA card.

Say: In today's story the brothers' jealousy causes a great deal of trouble in the family. God doesn't want us to be jealous of one another. God wants us to love one another.

Clothespin Tag

Supplies

spring clothespins, chairs, blankets or sheets

Move to an open area. Give each child a clothespin. Attach the clothespin to the back of his or her shirt or dress. Designate an area of the classroom to be the pit. The pit is made by putting chairs in a circle, the seats facing out. Make sure there is enough space for each child to sit in the pit, with his or her legs extended. Take several blankets or sheets and throw over the backs of the chairs, enclosing the circle.

Say: Each of you has one clothespin, but you want more. You don't just want your own; you want the ones that belong to the rest of the group. The object is for you to try to get the clothespin of someone else without someone getting yours. When your clothespin is gone, then you must go into the pit.

Start the game. When most of the children are in the pit, call the game.

When everyone is in the pit, **ask: How does it feel to be in the pit? Is it scary? exciting? Do you wonder what's going to happen?**

Say: Well, our Bible character for today probably had all those feelings. And how he got there was something terrible that his brothers did to him.

Sing the Story

Supplies

None

Sing together the song "When Jacob Gave Joseph a New Coat" to the tune of "My Bonnie Lies Over the Ocean."

When Jacob Gave Joseph a New Coat
(Tune: "My Bonnie Lies Over the Ocean")

When Jacob gave Joseph a new coat,
The new coat with colors so bright,
It made all the brothers so jealous,
That soon there would be a big fight.
Joseph, Joseph
Your new coat has colors so bright, so bright.
Joseph, Joseph,
Your new coat has colors so bright.

The brothers sent Joseph to Egypt
Right after the terrible fight.
But God was with Joseph in Egypt,
And everything turned out all right.
Joseph, Joseph,
Everything turned out all right, all right.
Joseph, Joseph,
Everything turned out all right.

God has a special plan for each of us.

Joseph, Man of the Year

by LeeDell Stickler

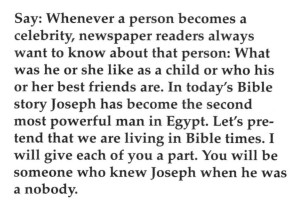

Say: Whenever a person becomes a celebrity, newspaper readers always want to know about that person: What was he or she like as a child or who his or her best friends are. In today's Bible story Joseph has become the second most powerful man in Egypt. Let's pretend that we are living in Bible times. I will give each of you a part. You will be someone who knew Joseph when he was a nobody.

You will need these parts: TV interviewer; the jailer; the cupbearer; the Pharaoh; the grain bearer; Ruben, one of Joseph's brothers; Simeon, another of Joseph's brothers; Benjamin, Joseph's youngest brother; Jacob; and Joseph's father.

Photocopy these pages and give each character his or her part.

TV Interviewer: Today we are celebrating the Man of the Year—Joseph. This man single-handedly saved Egypt. If it hadn't been for him, the whole country would have starved. But who is this man? Let's talk to some people who knew him before he was anyone special.

Jacob: Of course, as his father I loved Joseph. In fact I loved him more than any of my other eleven sons. I wanted to give him something special, something his eleven brothers didn't have, so I gave Joseph a beautiful coat with long sleeves.

Ruben: We were so mad about that coat. Joseph really thought he was better than the rest of us. He'd have these dreams that showed us bowing down to him. And he was a real tattletale, always running to our father. But we fixed him.

TV Interviewer: I understand there was an incident with a pit.

Simeon: Well, yes. We decided to get rid of Joseph, so when we were all out in the fields we took his new coat and threw Joseph into a pit. We dipped the coat in goat's blood and told our father that Joseph had been killed by a wild animal.

Ruben: But we actually sold Joseph to a caravan of traders on their way to Egypt.

TV Interviewer: I see. So that's how he wound up in Egypt. His files say that Potipher, the man who bought Joseph, put him in prison. Let's talk to some of those who knew him then.

Jailer: Joseph wasn't your typical prisoner. He was such a good-natured person. I put him in charge of the other prisoners.

Cupbearer: I think Joseph was arrested under false pretenses. One night I had a dream and I told Joseph about it. It seems as if he has this gift from God. Joseph can tell what dreams really mean. And everything he said was true. I was released and given my job back.

TV Interviewer: Cupbearer, it seems that you are primarily responsible for Joseph getting an early release from prison. Tell us what brought this about.

Cupbearer: I hadn't thought of Joseph for years. But one morning the Pharaoh had had a bad dream. No one could tell him what the dream meant. That's when I remembered Joseph. They fetched him from the prison ASAP.

TV Interviewer: How do you feel about him, Pharaoh?

Pharaoh: Joseph was a real lifesaver. Night after night I had the same dream. I knew someone was trying to send me a message, but I just didn't know what it was. But Joseph knew.

Grain bearer: I have hauled sacks and sacks of grain into those storehouses Joseph had us build. We've got enough food to last us for years and years. Of course, Joseph told us we were going to need this. He said the Pharaoh's dreams were predicting a time of famine.

TV Interviewer: Let's turn now to Joseph's youngest brother.

Benjamin: When the famine came my brothers went to Egypt to get food. They were surprised to find Joseph alive.

Ruben: He was the second most powerful man in Egypt. We could have been in big trouble. But Joseph forgave all of us.

TV Interviewer: Joseph, what do you have to say for yourself?

Joseph: God truly had a plan for my life. Because of what my brothers did, I was able to save the lives of many people. It was worth all the hard times.

Supplies

None

Parrot Talk

Have the children sit in a circle facing the teacher.

Say: I am going to say a sentence about the Bible story we heard. If it is true, then you will repeat it back to me. If it isn't true, then you will put your hand over your mouth.

Use these sentences:

Joseph had many brothers.
Joseph's brothers loved him very much. *(false)*
Joseph had a special coat.
Each of Joseph's brothers had a coat like his. *(false)*
Joseph had special dreams.
Joseph's dreams were about being President. *(false)*
Joseph was a tattletale.
His brothers threw him in a pit.
The brothers sold Joseph to an amusement park. *(false)*
The brothers sold Joseph to traders.
The traders were going to Florida. *(false)*
The brothers threw Joseph's coat away. *(false)*
Joseph spent time in prison.
Joseph helped other prisoners interpret their dreams.
Joseph help the Pharaoh interpret his dream.
The Pharaoh kept Joseph in prison. *(false)*
Joseph helped the people of Egypt get ready for a famine.
Joseph's brothers had plenty of food. *(false)*
Joseph's brothers came to Egypt to buy grain.
His brothers knew Joseph the minute they saw him. *(false)*
Joseph forgave his brothers.
Joseph knew that God had a plan for his life.

Supplies

None

Pharaoh Says

Have the children move to an open area of the room.

Say: In Egypt, the Pharaoh was the supreme ruler of the land. Whatever Pharaoh said had to be done.

Play "Pharaoh Says" like "Simon Says." Give directions such as "Pharaoh says, stand up." "Pharaoh says, touch your nose." "Turn around." If someone performs the action without your saying "Pharaoh says," just pause and say, "Oh, I caught some of you." Then begin again. To make the game more challenging and fun, give the instructions quickly.

God has a special plan for each of us.

Turn About Tales

Supplies

None

Bring the children together in the storytelling circle.

Say: Everybody loves a happy ending. At first we thought the story of Joseph was going to be a disaster. But it turned out happy. Let's see if we can give happy endings to these stories. I will give you the first part of the story. It will look like everything is lost. I want you to come up with a happy ending.

1. Jennifer and her mom were going on a picnic. But when Jennifer got up that morning, it was pouring down rain.
2. David and Jason were going to the movies. When they got there, the movie they wanted to see was sold out.
3. Elizabeth wanted to have her birthday party at Roller World. But her mother said the party would be too expensive.
4. The doctor told Stephen that from now on he would have to give up peanuts and chocolate. Every time he ate them, he broke out in a rash.
5. Joanie had saved her allowance to get a new video game. When she got to the store, they were all sold out of the ones she wanted.
6. Right before the championship soccer game, Heidi broke her ankle.

Prayer Signs

Supplies

None

Say: In today's Bible story we met a young man who first found himself as a slave, then a prisoner in jail, and then the governor of Egypt. Through it all, through the bad times and good times, he kept telling himself: My help comes from the Lord. We can tell ourselves that every day. Let's learn to sign that verse.

Teach the children the verse in American Sign Language. Let the children practice the verse until they can do it without looking.

Then pray: Dear God, whenever we have hard things to do, help us to remember *(Sign the verse)*. **Whenever we are feeling sick or hurt, help us to remember** *(Sign the verse)*. **Whenever things are not going our way, and we'd like to start all over again, help us to remember** *(Sign the verse)*. **Amen.**

REPRODUCIBLE 2A

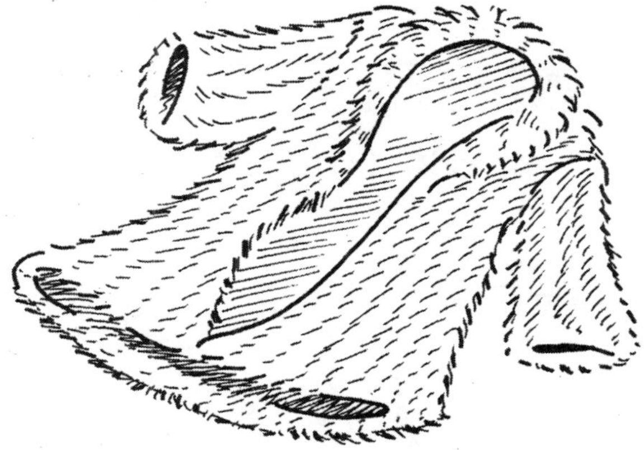

REPRODUCIBLE 2B

Ruth

Bible Verse

May the LORD reward you for your deeds.
Ruth 2:12

Bible Story

Ruth 1–4

The Book of Ruth helped the Jewish people establish the lineage of King David. In establishing the line the the book also pointed out that King David, Israel's most beloved king, was the grandson of a woman who was a foreigner and an immigrant.

In addition the story of Ruth also gives us some insight into the laws of the day, particularly those laws having to do with the relationships between the rich and the poor. According to Hebrew law, caring for the poor was not just a good thing to do, it was the law.

The economy of Israel at this time was primarily based on agriculture. According to the law, rich landowners were required to leave part of their harvest for people who were poor. Corners of fields were left untouched so that people who were poor could harvest some of the crop. After the harvest, the poor could also collect anything left in the field. This is called "gleaning."

Ruth had no obligation to Naomi, her mother-in-law, after the death of Ruth's husband. She easily could have returned to her own family and remarried at a later time. But Ruth loved Naomi and knew how difficult life was going to be for her. So Ruth chose to follow Naomi back to her homeland and to make sure Naomi has someone to care for her.

Children are egocentric but they can be loving and caring persons as well. They empathize with persons who are in need and often are moved to share what they have with them. The media has made our children more aware of the plight of the poor—not just in our own hometowns, but across the world. Help the children you teach recognize that God intends for us to care for persons who are poor and in need.

God wants us to be kind to others.

If time is limited, we recommend those activities that are noted in **boldface**. Depending on your time and the number of children, you may be able to include more activities.

Activity	Time	Supplies	
Harvest Time	**10 minutes**	**masking tape, newspaper, scissors, straws, optional: construction paper cut into one-inch strips**	Join the Fun
Grain Expectations	10 minutes	grains of barley, oats, and wheat (available at some local grocery stores or at food stores that specialize in organic foods); cutting board; smooth rock or meat hammer; plastic tablecloth or newspaper; wheat bread, barley bread, and oat bread; baskets	Bible Story Fun
Sing the Verse	5 minutes	None	
Bible Story: Where You Go, I Will Go	**10 minutes**	**None**	
Ruth's Road Rally	15 minutes	shoe box lids, white glue, pencils, chenille sticks, marbles	
Zedakah	10 minutes	Reproducible 3B, white glue or tape, crayons or scissors, felt-tip markers	
Make a Grain Chain	5 minutes	Reproducible 3A, scissors, tape or glue, felt-tip markers or crayons	Live the Fun
Echo Prayer	**5 minutes**	**None**	

Harvest Time

Supplies

masking tape, newspaper, scissors, straws, optional: construction paper cut into one-inch strips

Before the children arrive, mark off a square in the center of the room using masking tape. Make sure the square is at least ten feet on a side. (Make this square larger if you have a large class.) Mark a second square to the outside of this square (about one foot farther out).

Indicate the outside area as the red zone. Indicate the inside area as the yellow zone. Scatter straws (or construction paper cut into one-inch strips) around the two squares. Make sure there are straws or strips in both areas.

Greet the children as they arrive. Give each child a sheet of newspaper and some masking tape. Have the children create a basket from the newspaper. (Each child can create his or her own design.) As some children finish and other children arrive, let those who have finished assist the new arrivals.

Say: It's harvest time. It is our job to harvest all the straws we can find on the floor. I will assign areas. You may only gather in the area I assign.

Assign the majority of the children to the yellow zone. Assign a smaller number to the red zone.

Say: When I say "Go," let's see how much we can harvest.

When all the straws are picked up, have the children count the number of straws they have. Discover who has the largest number of straws and the smallest number of straws.

Then ask the children: Who had the most straws to gather? *(those in the yellow zone)* **Who had the fewest straws?** *(those in the red zone)* **What made the difference?** *(The people who harvested in the red zone has less area for straws.)* **If you were picking up gold coins or something very valuable, which area would you rather harvest?** *(the yellow zone)*

Say: In today's Bible story we hear about a special kind of harvesting called *gleaning*. In Bible times, the outside area of a field was left for the poor. The farmers wanted to make sure that even the poor people had food to eat. It was their way of being kind to others.

God wants us to be kind to others.

Grain Expectations

Supplies

grains of barley, oats, and wheat (available at some local grocery stores or at food stores that specialize in organic foods); cutting board; smooth rock or meat hammer; plastic tablecloth or newspaper; wheat bread, barley bread, and oat bread; baskets

Note: We do not believe in using food in a frivolous way. So the food items should be handled with care so that they can be used as originally intended. Keep waste to a minimum. Also, please check to see if any children have food allergies that would prevent them from tasting the grains or breads.

Cover the table with a plastic tablecloth or with newspaper. Place the wheat bread, barley bread, and oat bread into baskets.

Let the children examine kernels from each of the grains. Help the children match the grain to the breads.

Say: Barley, wheat, and oats were staples in the diet of the people of Bible times. They used these grains to make their breads. Bread was served in some fashion at every meal. If a person had bread, he or she didn't go hungry. Jesus used bread to symbolize his body at the Last Supper.

Let the children place several kernels of grain on the cutting board. Show the children how to use a smooth rock or meat hammer to crush the grain. Encourage the children to look at the flour that they are creating. Let the children taste the grain, the flour, and the bread.

Say: In our Bible story today, a woman named Ruth is picking grain to make bread so that she and her mother-in-law will have food to eat. Ruth is kind to her mother-in-law.

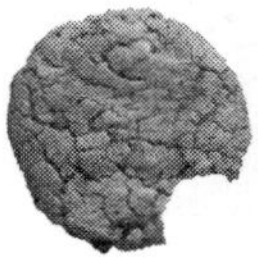

God wants us to be kind to others.

Sing the Verse

Supplies

None

Say: Today we are learning how people in Bible times showed kindness to others. Our Bible verse says, "May the Lord reward you for your deeds" (Ruth 2:12). Let's learn the Bible verse by singing.

Sing the verse to the tune of "Are You Sleeping?" Sing a phrase, and then have the children sing the phrase after you. Once the children learn the song, enjoy singing it as a round.

May the Lo-rd. May the Lo-rd.
Reward you. Reward you.
May the Lord reward you. May the Lord reward you.
For your deeds. For your deeds.

Where You Go, I Will Go

by LeeDell Stickler

Say: Today we are going to hear a story about a woman who, instead of taking the easy way, chose to take the way that was the most work. She would be going to a land where she would be known as a stranger and treated as a foreigner. But her loyalty was so strong, that she decided to do that anyway. She chose to do this because she was kind and loving.

When I signal, I want you to link arms with the person next to you and march in place. As you march in place you will say the short poem.

Together we will go
Movin' on down the road.
Arm and arm together,
We'll share each other's load.

"I am going to return home." said Naomi to Ruth and Orpah. "Since my husband and sons are dead there is no reason to stay here."

"Let us go with you," said Ruth.

"No, you and Orpah go back to your homes."

Together we will go
Movin' on down the road.
Arm and arm together,
We'll share each other's load.

"But we care about you and want to stay with you," said Orpah.

"No, you must go," said Naomi.

So Orpah hugged her mother-in-law and said good-bye. But Ruth stayed right where she was.

"Don't order me to leave," said Ruth. "Where you go, I will go. Your people will become my people. Your God will become my God."

So the two women began the journey to Bethlehem.

Together we will go
Movin' on down the road.
Arm and arm together,
We'll share each other's load.

When the two women arrived in Bethlehem, everyone rushed out to welcome them. "Is this Naomi who left here so long ago? Where is your husband? Where are your sons?" they asked.

"My husband and my sons are dead. That is why I have returned. All I have in the world is Ruth," said Naomi sadly.

So Ruth and Naomi settled into life in the village. Naomi had no one to provide a living for her. So if they were to eat, Ruth knew that she would be the one to go into the nearby fields and gather the grain.

The farmers from the village knew that caring for the poor was something God wanted them to do. So they would leave extra grain around the edges of the field and would allow the poor to gather it for their bread.

Together we will go
Movin' on down the road.
Arm and arm together,
We'll share each other's load.

Every morning Ruth hurried to the barley fields. All day long she gathered stalks of barley. She never stopped to rest or to talk with the workers.

One day Boaz, the owner of the field, noticed how hard Ruth worked. "Who is that woman?" he asked one of the workers.

"Her name is Ruth. She is Naomi's daughter-in-law," the worker said.

"I have heard of her. She takes care of Naomi. She is very kind," said Boaz, and he walked to where Ruth was working. "May the Lord reward you for your deeds. Stay in this field. I will make sure the workers leave enough grain for you and Naomi. When you get thirsty, share my water jars."

That night Ruth told Naomi all about Boaz. "Boaz is one of my relatives," said Naomi. "He would make a good husband for you. He would raise your sons as my grandsons. I think the two of you to should get married."

Naomi was a good matchmaker and Ruth and Boaz married.

Soon Ruth and Boaz had a new baby. They named him Obed. Naomi was a grandmother. Because of Ruth, Naomi would be lonely no longer.

Together we will go
Movin' on down the road.
Arm and arm together,
We'll share each other's load.

Ruth's Road Rally

Supplies

shoe box lids, white glue, pencils, chenille sticks, marbles

Say: Ruth and Naomi traveled to Bethlehem by themselves. Let's make a road rally maze to remind us of how hard the journey must have been.

Divide the children into teams of two or three. Give each team a shoebox lid, a set of ten chenille sticks (pipe cleaners), white glue, and a pencil.

Show them how to create a maze using the shoebox lid as the base. The chenille sticks will provide the sides of the path. Have the children sketch the path on the box lid and then glue the chenille sticks in place.

When the teams have their maze complete, give them a marble to run through the road rally.

Say: Ruth was kind to Naomi, and Boaz was kind to Ruth.

God wants us to be kind to others.

Zedakah

Supplies

Reproducible 3B, white glue or tape, crayons or scissors, felt-tip markers

Photocopy the money collectors **(Reproducible 3B)** for each child.

Say: Zedakah (ze DOCK ah) is a special Hebrew word that means acts of charity or kindness for the poor. When Boaz allowed Ruth to gather barley from his fields, he was performing an act of zedakah. When we make offerings for the poor, we perform acts of zedakah as well.

Select a giving project that the children can identify with. Heifer Project International (1 World Avenue, Little Rock, AR 72202) provides farm animals for persons and teaches them how to care for them. Write for information. Or involve the children in a project from the church.

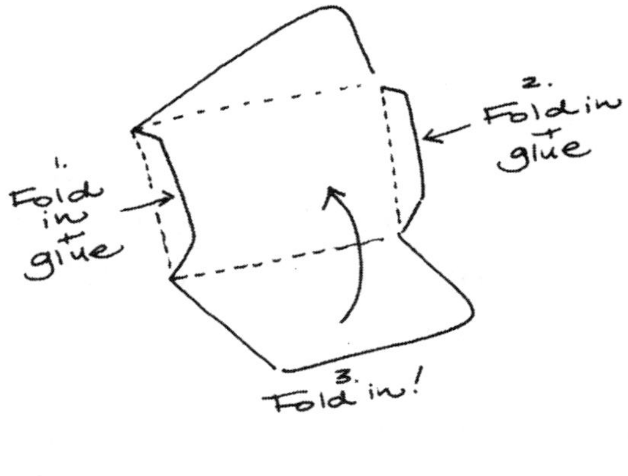

Encourage the children to decorate the money collectors with crayons or felt-tip markers. Have them cut out the envelopes and assemble as shown. Let the children take the money collectors home and bring them back at a designated time.

Say: God intended for the people to show kindness to the poor.

Make a Grain Chain

Photocopy the grain chain **(Reproducible 3A)** for each child.

Say: Another way we can be kind to others is by including them in our prayers. We are going to make a grain chain prayer reminder. Each night when we say our prayers, we remember to pray for those people listed on the chain.

Hand out the grain chain. Read the different things printed on the chains that the children will be praying for each night.

Encourage the children to color the strips. Then have the children make their paper chain by cutting out the strips and looping them around each other. Secure each strip with glue or tape.

Say: Hang the chain near your bed. As you say a bedtime prayer, count the loops and include the persons described.

Supplies

Reproducible 3A, scissors, tape or glue, felt-tip markers or crayons

God wants us to be kind to others.

Echo Prayer

Gather the children in a circle.

Say: I will say a phrase and I want your to repeat that phrase, just the way I said it.

Pray: *(in a loud happy voice)* **Thank you, God.**
(in a loud happy voice) **for family and friends.**
(in a whisper) **Thank you, God,**
(in an up and down pitch voice) **for food and shelter.**
(in a drawn-out voice) **Help me to remember**
(shout) **people!**
(in a normal voice) **People who have no family.**
(in a whisper) **People who have no friends.**
(in a deep voice) **People who need food and shelter.**
(very, very softly) **Amen.**

Supplies

None

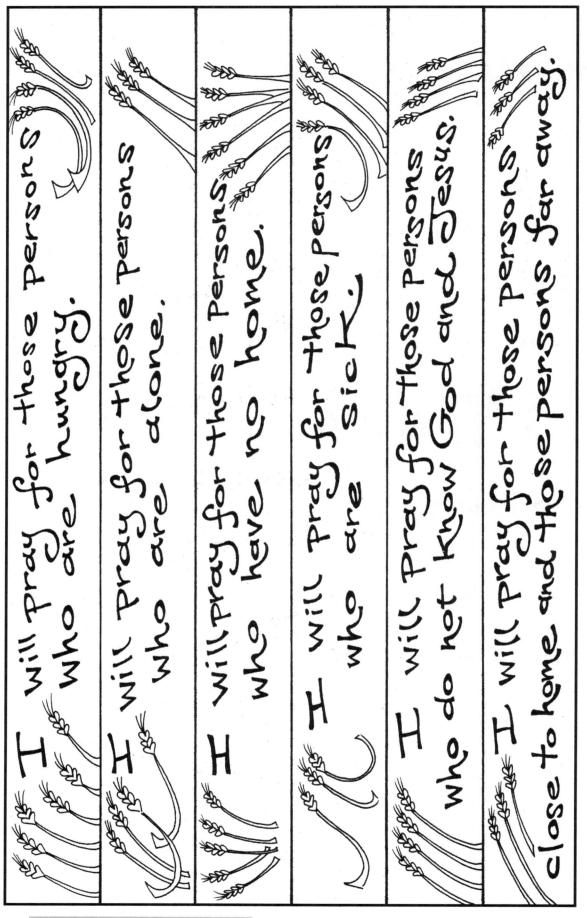

I will pray for those persons who are hungry.

I will pray for those persons who are alone.

I will pray for those persons who have no home.

I will pray for those persons who are sick.

I will pray for those persons who do not know God and Jesus.

I will pray for those persons close to home and those persons far away.

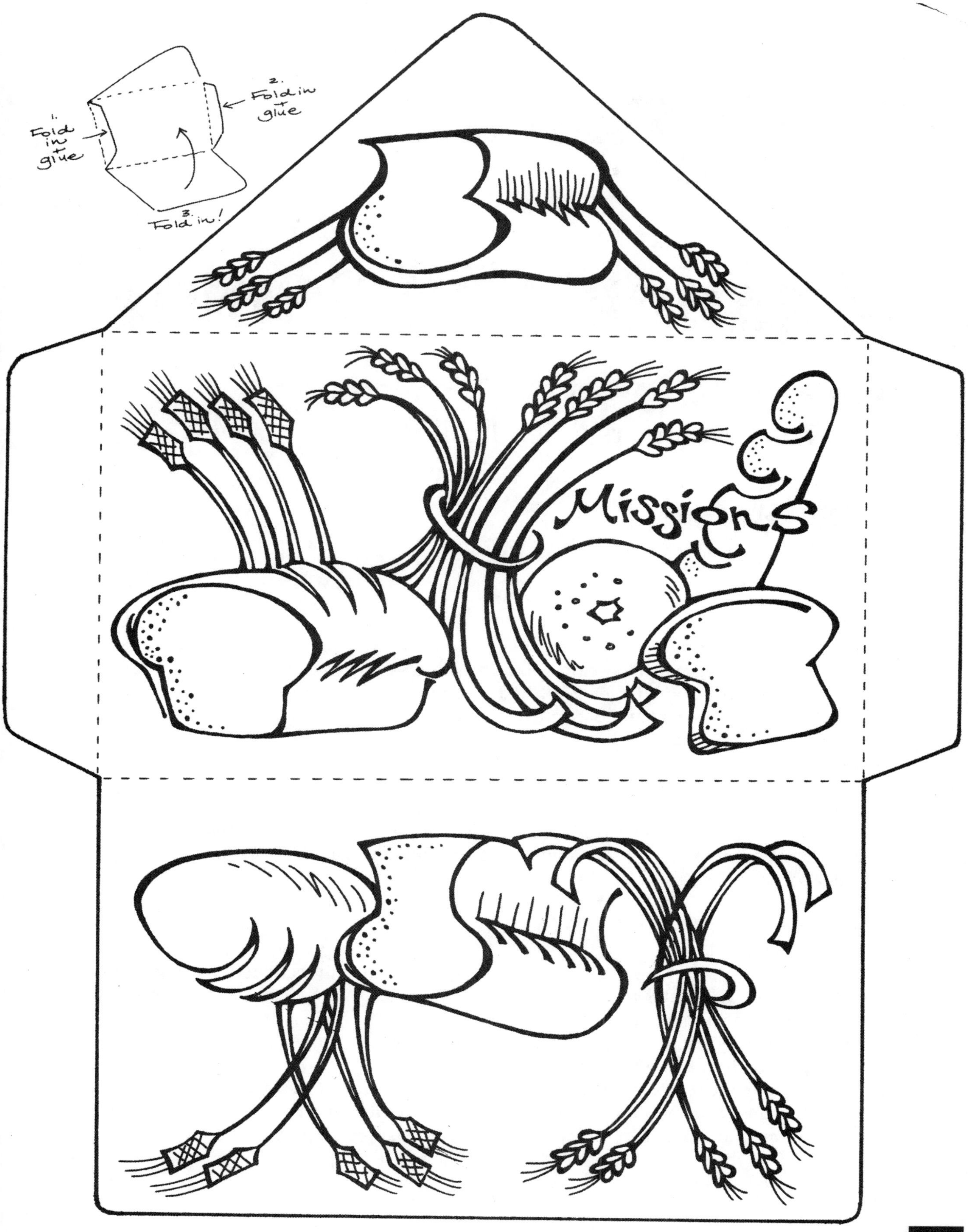

1. Fold in + glue
2. Fold in + glue
3. Fold in!
Missions

Lesson

4

All-in-One BIBLE FUN ELEMENTARY

Hannah and Samuel

Bible Verse

The LORD hears when I call to him.

Psalm 4:3

Bible Story

1 Samuel 1:1–2:10

At the time of this Bible story, the individual tribes of Israel had formed a loose organization called the Tribal Confederacy. They had no centralized government and depended upon judges to make God's will known to them. Eli, the priest in today's Bible story, was a judge in the town of Shiloh. The tribes also had established sanctuaries (temples) where people came to worship God. The Law required adult males to make a pilgrimage to a place of sanctuary at least three times a year. It was on one such pilgrimage that Hannah, wife of Elkanah (el-KAY-nuh), asked God for a child.

Hannah was barren. At this time in biblical culture a married woman who had not borne children was a source of scorn. Elkanah had sons by his other wife, Peninnah, and Peninnah made fun of Hannah. Yet Elkanah loved Hannah and tried in other ways to compensate for her lack of children.

Hannah was a woman of faith. She prayed for a son and promised to dedicate her child to God. God answered her prayers when she gave birth to a son whom she named Samuel, whose name means "asked of God."

Hannah nurtured Samuel until he was weaned, which was at about three years of age, according to the culture of the day. Then she fulfilled her promise to God and joyfully dedicated her son to the Lord.

For Hannah this dedication meant that Samuel had been set apart from others for the special purpose of serving God. She vowed that Samuel would live a holy consecrated life as a Nazirite and a minister in the temple. Being a Nazirite meant that Samuel was dedicated to lifelong service to God.

Talk to your children about prayer. Help them understand that prayer is not magical. God answers all prayers, but not always in the way we expect.

We can ask God to help us.

If time is limited, we recommend those activities that are noted in **boldface**. Depending on your time and the number of children, you may be able to include more activities.

Activity	Time	Supplies	
A Special Place to Pray	10 minutes	pillows, table, scissors, tape, crepe paper, large appliance box, utility knife (adult use only), felt-tip markers, optional: glow-in-the dark stars	Join the Fun
Sacred Chest	**10 minutes**	**Reproducible 4A, felt-tip markers or crayons**	
I Need A Little Help!	5 minutes	resealable plastic bags, water, treats, chairs	Bible Story Fun
Prayer Wave	5 minutes	None	
Bible Story: Hannah's Prayer	**10 minutes**	**None**	
I Promise	10 minutes	Reproducible 4B, scissors, newsprint, construction paper, felt-tip markers, stapler and staples	
Four Kinds of Prayer	5 minutes	four large sheets of paper, felt-tip marker	
Praying Hands	10 minutes	plain paper, pencils, scissors, shallow pan, water	Live the Fun
Prayer Steps	**5 minutes**	**None**	

Supplies

pillows, table, scissors, tape, crepe paper, large appliance box, utility knife (adult use only), felt-tip markers, optional: glow-in-the dark stars

A Special Place to Pray

Say: I need your help today. I want to add a special place to our room where we can sit and quietly pray.

Plan to use a taller table. Invite the children to tape strips of crepe paper to the top of the table so that they hang down like curtains. Let the children place pillows underneath the table.

Or, provide a large appliance box. Before the children arrive use a utility knife to cut a door into the box. Let the children decorate the outside of the box with felt-tip markers. Add glow-in-the dark star stickers to the inside of the box or encourage the children to draw stars on the ceiling and walls inside the box. Add pillows to the floor of the box.

Say: Today our story is about a woman named Hannah. Hannah was deeply sad. She went to a special place to pray and ask God for help. We can use this special place in our room as one place we can pray. We can pray in special places or anywhere we happen to be.

Invite the children to try out the special place for prayer.

Supplies

Reproducible 4A, felt-tip markers or crayons

Sacred Chest

Photocopy the dot-to-dot picture **(Reproducible 4A)** for each child.

Say: When you follow the dots, you'll find the sacred chest. The sacred chest, also known as the ark of the covenant, was a box or chest. According to biblical tradition, the chest held the Ten Commandments. The chest was kept in the temple, a special place to worship God. Today's story is about a woman named Hannah and her husband, Elkanah. Every year Elkanah went with his family to the temple. This year Hannah went into the temple to ask God for help.

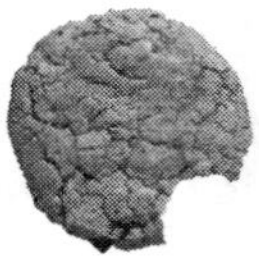

We can ask God to help us.

Encourage the children to complete the dot-to-dot pictures and then decorate the pictures with crayons or markers. Display the pictures in your special prayer area or in your story area.

I Need a Little Help!

Supplies

resealable plastic bags, water, treats, chairs

Have the children form pairs. Have the pairs put their chairs back to back and sit in them. One will be "A" and the other, "B." Give each team a resealable plastic bag filled with water.

Say: You look like a strong bunch of boys and girls. I'm going to challenge you. If your team can hold this plastic bag filled with water over your head, then we will all get treats. It sounds easy, but you have to hold it up for three minutes. Now, just in case you need help, your partner can reach up and take it from you. All you have to say is "I need a little help!" Your partner will take over. When your partner needs help, he or she can say the same thing.

Even though the children are sitting down, holding a bag of water overhead will be a lot harder than it appears.

Ask: How many of you needed help holding the bag of water overhead? How did if feel when you were able to turn it over to your partner? *(a relief)*

Say: In today's Bible story a woman named Hannah is very troubled and needs help. She asks God to be her partner and help.

We can ask God to help us.

Prayer Wave

Supplies

None

Have the children sit in a circle. Remind the children of today's Bible verse: "The LORD hears when I call to him" (Psalm 4:3).

Say: Let's have a prayer wave. I will begin the Bible verse by standing up and saying the first word. Then I will sit down. The next person will stand up, say the second word of the Bible verse, and then sit down. The third person will stand up, say the third word of the Bible verse, and then sit down. Let's see how many times we can go around the circle.

Practice one or two times until the children get the hang of it. Encourage the children to do the wave and say the verse faster and faster.

Hannah's Prayer

by LeeDell Stickler

Have the children listen for the feelings expressed in this story. If the feeling is happy, have the children shout "Yes!". If the feeling is sad, have the children pretend to cry.

After telling the story lead the children in singing "Hannah" to the tune of "The Farmer in the Dell."

Elkanah and his family lived in Ramah, a town in the hill country of Ephraim. Elkanah had two wives—Peninnah and Hannah. They were all very **happy** *(Yes!)*—except for Hannah *(cry)*. Peninnah had children but Hannah had none. Hannah was **sad** because she had no children *(cry)*.

Once a year Elkanah traveled from his hometown to Shiloh, where he worshiped the Lord All Powerful and made sacrifices. It was a **happy** time *(Yes!)*, because the whole family would go.

One day while the family was in Shiloh, Hannah felt so **sad** *(cry)* she began to cry. She refused to eat. She really wanted a child of her own.

Elkanah asked her, "Why are you **sad**?" *(cry)* Why won't you eat? Don't I mean more to you than ten sons?"

Hannah loved Elkanah very much, but she still wanted a child of her own. After all the sacrifices had been made and the meal eaten, Hannah went into the place of worship to pray.

Hannah prayed with all her heart, "Lord All Powerful, I am your servant. But I am so **sad** *(cry)*. Please let me have a son. I will give him to you for as long as he lives."

Hannah prayed and prayed and prayed. When she ran out of words, she prayed even more. In fact, her lips moved and not a sound came out.

Eli the priest was watching her. Here was a woman moving her lips without making a sound. She must be drunk, he thought to himself! "Woman," he said sternly, "How long will you stay drunk! Sober up!"

"Please sir," Hannah answered. "I'm not drunk. But I do feel **sad** *(cry)*. I've been praying all this time, asking God to help me."

Eli came to where Hannah was kneeling. "Go home now and stop being **sad** *(cry)*. I'm sure the God of Israel will answer your prayer."

"Thank you for being so kind to me," Hannah answered. Then she left. She felt so much better. She was almost **happy** *(Yes!)*.

The next morning Elkanah and Hannah and Peninnah went home. Sure enough Hannah and Elkanah soon had a child of their own. Now Hannah was **happy** *(Yes!)*.

"Samuel," said Hannah to her baby son, "you are a gift from God. One day I will take you back to the temple in Shiloh. I will keep my promise to God."

Four years later, when Elkanah and Hannah and Peninnah made the trip to Shiloh, Samuel went with them. After Elkanah made sacrifices for Samuel, Hannah brought the boy to the priest Eli.

"A few years ago I stood here at this place of worship and asked God for a child," said Hannah. "Here he is! I am giving him to the Lord, as he will be the Lord's servant for as long as he lives. Hannah was very **happy** *(Yes!)*.

Hannah
(Tune: "The Farmer in the Dell")

O Hannah prayed to God.
O Hannah prayed to God.
She prayed that she would
have a son.
O Hannah prayed to God.

O Hannah had a son.
O Hannah had a son.
She had a son named Sam-u-el
O Hannah had a son.

Words: Daphna Flegal and Judy Newman-St. John

I Promise

Supplies

Reproducible 4B, scissors, newsprint, construction paper, felt-tip markers, stapler and staples

Photocopy the promise strips **(Reproducible 4B)** for each child.

Say: Hannah made a promise to God. She promised that if she had a son, he would serve the Lord. When Hannah had Samuel, she kept her promise and dedicated him to God.

Ask: What are some things we can promise God? *(to be kind to my little brother, to do what my parents say to do, to help others, to pray every day, to love God, to serve God, and so forth)*

Help the children make a list on newsprint.

Say: Let's make a promise coupon book. We can fill the book and keep it as a reminder of what we promised God.

Have the children make a construction paper cover for the book. Then have the children cut out the coupons and staple them inside. Help the children fill in their coupons.

Four Kinds of Prayer

Supplies

four large sheets of paper, felt-tip marker

Say: When we pray, we can pray different kinds of prayers. One kind is an asking prayer. *(Write "Asking" on a sheet of paper.)* **Hannah asked God to give her a baby. What might we ask for?** *(Write two or three suggestions in the form of simple prayers. For example, if food is mentioned, write, "Please give us food to eat.")*

Say: Another kind of prayer is a thank-you prayer. *(Write "Thank You" on a second sheet of paper.)* **Hannah thanked God when baby Samuel was born. What can we thank God for?** *(Write two or three prayers, such as "Thank you, God, for food.")*

Say: Another kind of prayer is an "I'm sorry" prayer that asks God for forgiveness. *(Write "I'm Sorry" on a third sheet of paper.)* **Eli could have prayed, "I'm sorry that I thought Hannah was behaving strangely." What "I'm sorry" prayers can we pray?** *(Write two or three prayers, such as, "I'm sorry I hit my brother.")*

Say: A fourth kind of prayer is a prayer asking help for others. *(Write "Help for Others" on the last sheet of paper.)* **Hannah asked God to look after Samuel when she was not with him. Who can we pray for and ask God to help?** *(Write two or three of the answers as prayers, such as "Help my grandmother get well.")*

Praying Hands

Supplies

plain paper, pencils, scissors, shallow pan, water

Give each child a piece of plain paper to make a handprint. Have each child place a hand on the paper. Be sure that the child has his or her fingers spread apart. Encourage the children to work together to trace one another's hand.

Have the children cut out their handprints. Then have them write something in each finger's outline that they would like God to help them with such as being kinder to a younger brother, remembering to practice spelling words, or helping grandmother feel better.

Say: Today our Bible story is about a woman named Hannah. Hannah prayed to God and asked for God's help.

We can ask God to help us.

When the children have completed their handprints, have them fold the fingers down into the palm.

Let the children take turns floating each handprint in a shallow pan of water. The fingers will unfold.

Say: Remember—God hears and answers all prayers.

Prayer Steps

Supplies

None

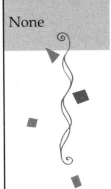

Have the children form a prayer circle, holding hands behind their backs instead of in front.

Say: I will say a phrase, and you will repeat it, taking one step to the right. Then I will say a phrase, and you will repeat it, taking one step to the left. We will move back and forth while we say the four different kinds of prayers.

Use these phrases:

Dear God, please help us *(Children repeat and move one step to the right.)*
show love to others. *(Children repeat and move one step to the left.)*
Thank you, God, *(Children repeat and move one step to the right.)*
for our families. *(Children repeat and move one step to the left.)*
We are sorry for the times *(Children repeat and move one step to the right.)*
we have been unkind. *(Children repeat and move one step to the left.)*
Please help our families *(Children repeat and move one step to the right.)*
stay safe and well. Amen. *(Children repeat and move one step to the center.)*

REPRODUCIBLE 4A

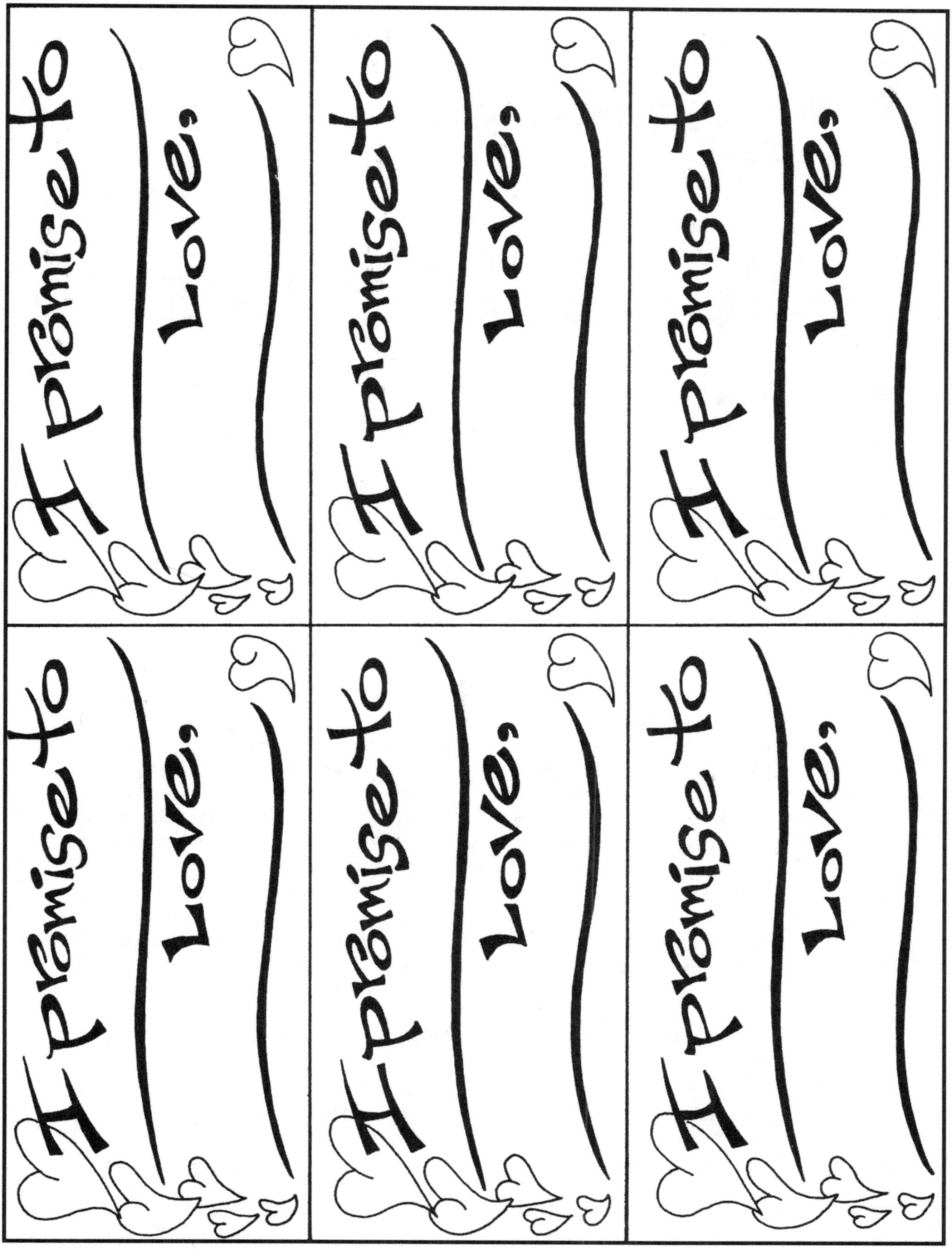

REPRODUCIBLE 4B

Lesson

5 All-in-One BIBLE ELEMENTARY FUN

Samuel Listens

Bible Verse

I'm listening, LORD. What do you want me to do?

1 Samuel 3:9, CEV

Bible Story

1 Samuel 3:1-19

Hannah kept the promise she made to God. Surely she must have felt that Samuel had been chosen by God for some special purpose. In sharp contrast to Hannah's delight with her son was Eli's despair over his sons. Time and time again they showed complete disregard for God's laws. According to the customs of the day, the priesthood should have passed from Eli to his descendants, but because of the moral and cultic violations committed by Eli's sons, God withdrew the blessing from the house of Eli.

Although Samuel stayed on as Eli's assistant in the temple at Shiloh, Hannah and Elkanah remained faithful to their son. Each year they visited him when they came to worship in the temple, and Hannah brought him a new cloak she had made. God continued to bless Hannah, and she bore five more sons.

Although still young, Samuel took an active role in service in the temple. His duties in the temple likely would have included filling and lighting the lamp, which played an important part in religious practices. Opening and closing the temple doors probably meant more than just the physical act; travelers likely were asking the young man for advice. Still Samuel had not had a personal experience with God.

When God first spoke to Samuel, Samuel assumed it was Eli calling him. It took an older, experienced Eli to realize finally that the voice Samuel was hearing was God's.

After the visit from God the focus began to shift from Eli to Samuel. In time Samuel became a great leader, prophet, and priest. He was respected by the people and favored by God.

Help your children understand that God speaks to us in many ways. Be a model of God's love and acceptance for them.

God calls us to serve others.

If time is limited, we recommend those activities that are noted in **boldface**. Depending on your time and the number of children, you may be able to include more activities.

ACTIVITY	TIME	SUPPLIES	
On the Line	**10 minutes**	**paper cups, paper clips, sharpened pencil, string, crayons**	JOIN THE FUN
Listen Up!	10 minutes	masking tape, whistle	
Sound Effects	5 minutes	Reproducible 5A, scissors, small box or basket	BIBLE STORY FUN
Bible Story: I'm Listening, Lord	**10 minutes**	**four towels, or blankets, or signs**	
Pass the Word	5 minutes	None	
How Do You Know?	5 minutes	None	
Scripture Scroll	5 minutes	Reproducible 5B, crayons or felt-tip markers, scissors, ribbon or yarn	LIVE THE FUN
Prayer Squeeze	**5 minutes**	**None**	

On the Line

Supplies

paper cups, paper clips, sharpened pencil, string, crayons

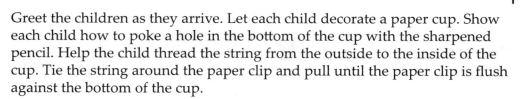

Each pair of children will need two paper cups, a 10- to 15-foot length of string, and two paper clips.

Greet the children as they arrive. Let each child decorate a paper cup. Show each child how to poke a hole in the bottom of the cup with the sharpened pencil. Help the child thread the string from the outside to the inside of the cup. Tie the string around the paper clip and pull until the paper clip is flush against the bottom of the cup.

Have the teams hold their cups and walk apart until the string is taut. One child will put the cup to his or her ear. The other child will put the cup to his or her mouth and talk. The sound vibrations will travel down the string, and the children have a version of a telephone.

Say: In today's lesson someone receives a call from God.

Ask: Do you think it is a telephone call? How do you think God talks to people? What would you say if God spoke to you?

God calls us to serve others.

Listen Up!

Supplies

masking tape, whistle

Bring the children together in an open area. Create a safety zone in an area of the room. Mark it with masking tape.

Say: When we are listening for God's call, we had better be good listeners. Let's play a game and see just how good you are at listening and following directions. One of you will be the "Caller." The rest of you will be part of the group. Over there is an area called the safety zone. In the safety zone, you can't be tagged. In this game we are going to form groups of different sizes. You will have listen very carefully and pay attention. When I say, "Sprawl," everyone will begin to hop around until you hear the whistle blow. Then the Caller will call out a number between two and five. Run to form groups of that number before you are tagged by the Caller. If you're left without a group, run to the safety zone. The first person tagged becomes the next Caller.

Ask: Was it fun to play the game? Did you have to listen very carefully? What happened if you didn't listen? *(You got caught without a group.)*

Sound Effects

Supplies

Reproducible 5A, scissors, small box or basket

Photocopy and cut apart the sound effects pictures **(Reproducible 5A)** and put them in a basket.

Have the children come to the storytelling area and sit on the floor.

Say: Everything has a unique sound, a sound all its own. I am going to call each of you to the front one at a time. You will draw a sound effects card and make that sound. The rest of the class will try to guess what object you are.

When everyone has had a chance to make the sound of his or her picture, have the children participate in the following story.

One day Clarence the Duck *(sound effect)* **went out for a walk. As he walked, he ran into his friend Bubba the Dog** *(sound effect)*. **The two decided that it was a very nice day for a stroll. Clarence** *(sound effect)* **pulled his flute** *(sound effect)* **from his pocket and began to play. Bubba** *(sound effect)* **thought that music was just the ticket, so he took out his trumpet and begin to play as the friends walked along.**

Just then Clarence and Bubba turned the corner and ran smack into Sybil the Cat *(sound effect)*. **Sybil was sitting on the lawn playing her guitar** *(sound effect)*. **As Sybil** *(sound effect)* **strummed, Bert the Bird** *(sound effect)* **whistled a merry tune. All four friends agreed that this was indeed a lovely day.**

Just then Milton the Mouse *(sound effect)* **came running up to them. "Didn't you hear the bell** *(sound effect)*?**" Milton** *(sound effect)* **squeaked. "Lightning** *(sound effect)* **struck an airplane** *(sound effect)* **that was flying overhead. The airplane** *(sound effect)* **had to land on the road. The fire engines** *(sound effect)* **are there to make sure no one is hurt."**

All three friends agreed that it had been an exciting day.

Say: You had to listen as I told this story in order to make the correct sound effect. Listening is important in our Bible story today. In this story, a boy named Samuel listens as God calls him by name.

God calls us to serve others.

I'm Listening, Lord

by LeeDell Stickler

Designate four areas in the room: the temple, the home, Samuel's bed, and Eli's bed. Spread blankets or, if your class is small, large beach towels on the floor in these areas. If your class is large, simply mark the areas with a sign.

Say: During the story there is a lot of traveling going on. And we are going to travel with the travellers. Sometimes we will travel to the temple. *(Have the children move to the temple area.)* **Sometimes we will go home.** *(Have the children move back to home.)* **Sometimes we will run to see Eli.** *(Move to Eli's bed.)* **Sometimes we will go back to sleep.** *(Move to Samuel's bed.)* **Let's begin.**

(Move to home.)
Hannah prayed and prayed for a son. God answered Hannah's prayer and Hannah gave birth to a boy. Hannah named her son Samuel.

(Everyone go to the temple.) When Samuel was older, Hannah brought him to the priest Eli. "I am here to keep my promise to God. I told God that if I could have a son, I would dedicate him to God. I have brought Samuel to you."

(Everyone goes home.)
Hannah and Elkanah returned to their home. Samuel stayed behind at the temple to help Eli. Eli would raise Samuel to be a servant of God.

Every day Samuel would get up. He would open the doors to the sanctuary. He would fill the lamp cups with oil. Whatever Eli asked of him, Samuel would do.

One night Samuel laid down on he sleeping mat. He had just barely closed his eyes when he heard a voice: "Samuel! Samuel! Samuel! Samuel!"

Samuel sat up and looked about him. There was no one there, so it must be Eli calling him. Samuel jumped up and ran to where Eli was sleeping. *(Everyone move to Eli's space.)*

"Here I am, Eli. What do you want?" Eli looked truly surprised to find the boy standing there.

"Samuel, I did not call you. You must have been dreaming. Go back to bed!" So Samuel returned to his sleeping mat. *(Everyone return to Samuel's place.)*

Samuel laid back down and closed his eyes. Again he heard someone calling his name: "Samuel! Samuel!"

Samuel jumped up and ran to where Eli was sleeping. *(Everyone get up and move to Eli's space.)*

"Here I am. What do you want?" Samuel asked. Again Eli seemed puzzled that Samuel was there.

"You must be dreaming, Samuel. I did not call you. Go back to sleep," said Eli. And Samuel returned to his sleeping mat. *(Everyone return to Samuel's place.)*

One more time Samuel went back to his bed. He laid down on his mat and his closed his eyes. One more time he heard someone calling his name: "Samuel, Samuel!"

One more time Samuel jumped up and ran to Eli. *(Everyone move to Eli's space.)*

By this time Eli knew that something strange was going on. *Hmm,* he thought to himself. *God must be trying to speak to Samuel.* Eli scratched his chin and tried to decide what to do.

"Samuel, I did not call you. Go back to bed. The next time you hear the voice calling your name, answer, 'I'm listening, Lord. What do you want me to do?'"

And Samuel went back to his sleeping mat. *(Everyone return to Samuel's place.)*

Samuel laid back down and stared at the ceiling. "Samuel, Samuel!" the voice called out.

But instead of running to Eli, Samuel sat up and said, "I'm listening, Lord. What do you want me to do?"

That night God and Samuel began a lifelong conversation. For Samuel served God for the rest of his days.

Pass the Word

Supplies

None

Have the children form a circle on the floor or in chairs.

Say: I am going to give you a special message. I will whisper it in someone's ear. That person will pass the message to the next person, who will pass the message to the next person. We will keep passing the message until it is all the way around the circle. Listen carefully. We don't want to send a wrong message.

Here are some suggested messages: "Say your prayers." "Share with others." "Help one another." "Tell someone about Jesus." Invite the children to share the message that gets around. Point out how easily it can get distorted.

Play the game one more time using the Bible verse: "Speak, LORD, for your servant is listening" (1 Samuel 3:9).

How Do You Know?

Supplies

None

Ask: How did God talk to Samuel? *(Samuel heard God's voice.)* **How does God talk to us?** *(Invite the children to share how they think God can talk to us today.)* **How do we know what God wants us to do?**

Say: We can listen for God's voice. Sometimes we can hear God as we read the Bible. Sometimes we can hear God as we listen to Sunday school teachers or pastors. Sometimes we hear God through loving adults who care for us.

Say: I am going to name some things that boys and girls can do. If you think that these are things that God might call us to do, hold your hand like a telephone *(thumb and pinky finger extended, middle three fingers folded down)* **and say, "Ringy dingy." If you think it is something that God definitely would not call us to do, then make the rejection buzzer sound. If an activity is neither one, shrug your shoulders.**

1. Volunteer to help with Special Olympics on Saturday. *(ringy dingy)*
2. Skip church and go swimming instead. *(buzzer)*
3. Go to the movies on Sunday afternoon. *(shrug)*
4. Collect blankets for the homeless. *(ringy dingy)*
5. Spread a rumor about a classmate. *(buzzer)*
6. Participate in a charity walk-a-thon. *(ringy dingy)*
7. Play with friends in the park. *(shrug)*
8. Spend your church money on ice cream. *(buzzer)*
9. Do extra chores for your grandmother, who's sick. *(ringy dingy)*
10. Laugh at the weird clothes of a new kid in school. *(buzzer)*

Scripture Scroll

Supplies

Reproducible 4B, crayons or felt-tip markers, scissors, ribbon or yarn

Photocopy the Scripture scroll **(Reproducible 5B)** for each child.

Say: In Bible days the Bible was written on a scroll. The scroll was a long sheet that was rolled for easy reading and storage. Let's make a Scripture scroll with our Bible verse printed on it.

Give each child a copy of the scroll. Have the children read the Bible verse together. Point out the illuminated "I" explaining that this is Samuel, who listened to God. Have the children decorate the letter "I" with crayons or felt-tip markers.

Let the children crumple their scrolls and then spread them smooth again. Have the children repeat this process several times. This will make the paper look like old parchment.

Have the children cut lengths of ribbon or yarn into 12-inch pieces. Let the children roll their scrolls and tie them with a ribbon or piece of yarn.

Prayer Squeeze

Supplies

None

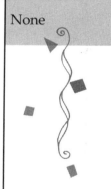

Bring the children together in a group. Have the children form a circle holding hands, crossing their right arms over their left arms.

Say: Let's close today with a friendship circle prayer. I will say a sentence, and you will respond with our Bible verse: "I'm listening, Lord. What do you want me to do?" Then I will begin a gentle squeeze and I want each of you to pass the squeeze around the circle. When it gets back to me, I will add another line to our prayer. You will respond with the Bible verse.

Pray: Thank you, God, for always listening to our prayers. *("I'm listening, Lord. What do you want me to do?")* **Thank you for the Bible and the stories that help us know what you want us to do.** *("I'm listening, Lord. What do you want me to do?")* **We pray for our pastor, our teacher, our parents, and all the people we know who help us know what you want us to do.** *("I'm listening, Lord. What do you want me to do?")* **We know you call us to love and serve others.** *("I'm listening, Lord. What do you want me to do?")* **Amen.**

God calls us to serve others.

REPRODUCIBLE 5A

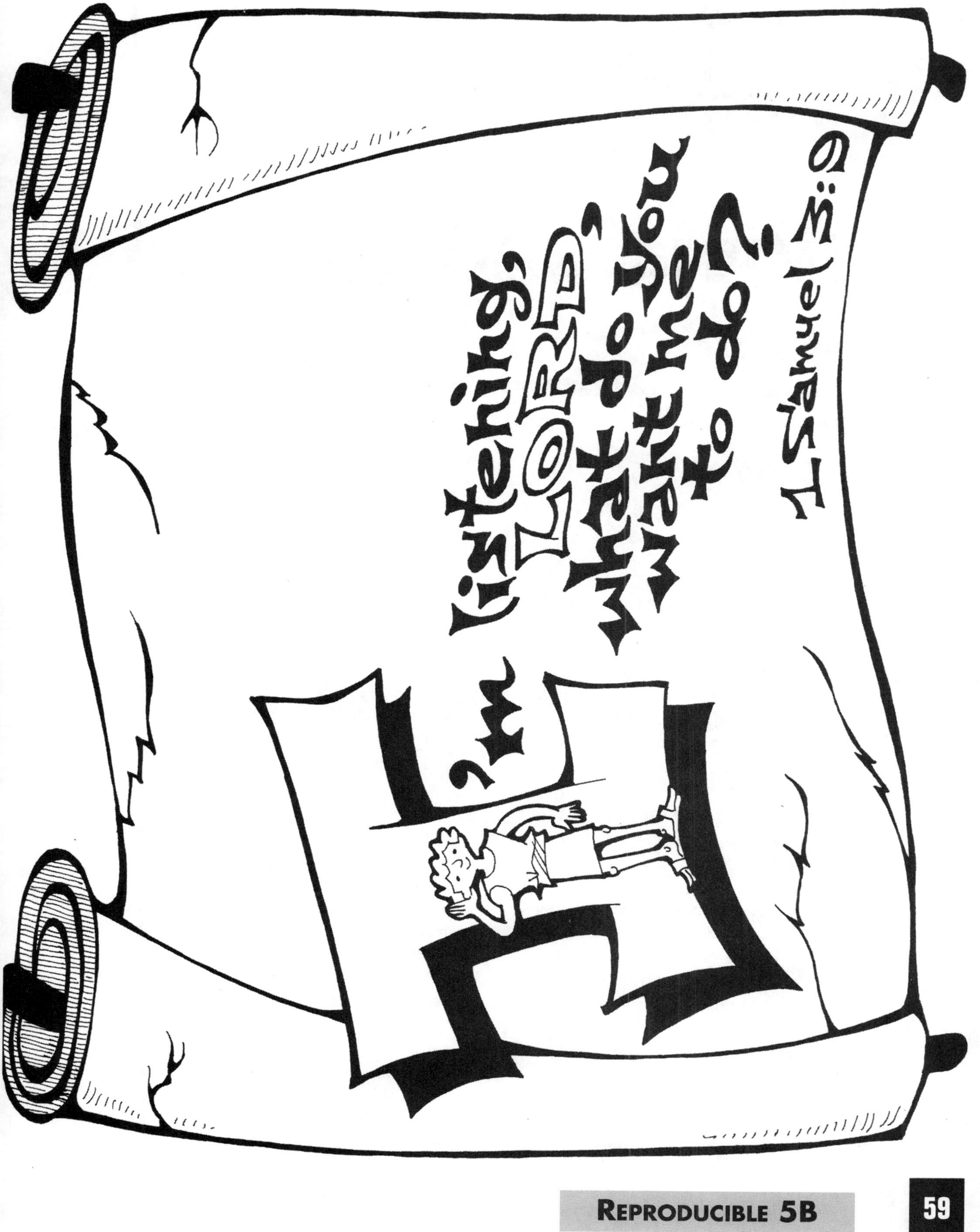
I'm listening, LORD, what do you want me to do?
1 Samuel 3:9

Lesson
6
All-in-One BIBLE FUN ELEMENTARY

David and Samuel

Bible Verse

The LORD looks on the heart.

1 Samuel 16:7

Bible Story

1 Samuel 16:1–13

Begrudgingly, at the people's demand, God had chosen a leader for Israel. But Saul's devotion to God was not as strong as Samuel's had been. Saul was a soldier. His downfall came when he put his wants and needs ahead of God's commands. The war with the Amalekites was a holy war, and God had commanded Saul to sacrifice all the spoils of war to God. Instead, Saul allowed his men to keep the best for their own personal use. Samuel saw Saul's disobedience as a rejection of God.

Saul tried to recover his kingly prestige, but he failed. Samuel knew the time had come for Israel to have a new king—one who would be faithful to God and who would give complete obedience.

Surely Samuel had some reservations when God sent him out to the little town of Bethlehem to find the next king. Had Saul known of Samuel's errand, Saul would certainly have had Samuel killed. So Samuel went to Bethlehem under a trumped-up mission. It was there among Jesse's sons that God had found the next king of Israel.

How often do we decide we like or don't like someone by the way he or she looks? Everyone is probably guilty of this at one time or another. Even children evaluate persons by their surface appearance. A person who is different is likely to be the class "nerd" or at the very least the class outcast. Once classified these people become the least admired by the children themselves. Adult attitudes often can affect these feelings. How often do we hear children parroting comments they have overheard from parents that they could not possibly understand?

Our responsibility as teachers is to help our children recognize that it is the inward person who is important. Each of us is a child of God just because we breathe. God loves each of us just as we are.

God loves us just as we are.

If time is limited, we recommend those activities that are noted in **boldface**. Depending on your time and the number of children, you may be able to include more activities.

Activity	Time	Supplies	
Hearts a'Plenty	**5 minutes**	**Reproducible 6A, red crayons or felt-tip markers**	Join the Fun
What Do You See?	10 minutes	mirrors, pencils, multicultural crayons, drawing paper	
Inside-Out Bags	10 minutes	Reproducible 6B, paper lunch bags, scissors, pencils, crayons or felt-tip markers, tape or glue, scale, tape measure, stapler and staples, ball	Bible Story Fun
Bible Story: You're the One!	**10 minutes**	**None**	
Who's the One?	10 minutes	None	
Body Boggled	10 minutes	chairs	
Affirmations and Prayer	**10 minutes**	**ball, optional: CD and CD player**	Live the Fun

Supplies

Reproducible 6A, red crayons or felt-tip markers

Hearts a'Plenty

Photocopy the hidden picture sheet **(Reproducible 6A)** for each child.

Greet the children as they come in. Direct them to a table where the hidden picture sheets have been set out. Let them try to see how many hearts they can find in the picture. Have them color the hearts red.

Say: Today we are going to talk about how God knows us inside out and loves us as we are.

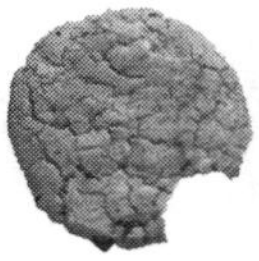

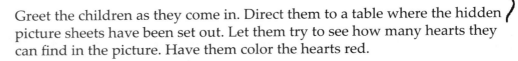

God loves us just as we are.

Supplies

mirrors, pencils, multicultural crayons, drawing paper

What Do You See?

Put the children into groups of two. Give each child a sheet of drawing paper and a pencil. Give each pair a small mirror.

Say: Draw an oval for your face. Begin by drawing an oval in the air several times. Then lightly draw the oval on your paper. Go around the oval several times. Then trace over the oval with a darker line.

Have the children look in the mirrors or use your own face as an example. Encourage the children to draw self-portraits as you describe how to draw a face.

Say: Look at your face in the mirror (*or, Look at my face*). Where are your eyes positioned between the bottom of your chin and the top of your forehead? They are in the middle. The width across your face measures five eyes wide. Now look at your nose. Where is the bottom of your nose? It is halfway between your eyes and the bottom of your chin. Now look at where your mouth is positioned between the bottom of your nose and your chin. It is in the middle. Notice the width of your mouth. Your mouth is as wide as the pupils (black dot in each eye) in your eyes. Now look at your ears. Where do the top of your ears begin? The ears start at the same level as the eyebrows. Where do the bottoms of your ears end? The ears stop at the same level as the bottom of the nose.

Ask: Your self-portrait shows the you that is on the outside, but does it tell us what kind of person you are? are you kind? are you loving?

Say: In today's Bible story, we learn that God doesn't look at the outside of a person. God sees the heart, the inside of a person.

Inside-Out Bags

Photocopy the hearts **(Reproducible 6B)** for each child.

Say: Most of the time we only get to know the outside of a person. We know what they look like, what they sound like. But, unless we are very good friends, we may not know what they are like on the inside. Today we are going to make Inside-Out Bags.

Say: Each of you will have ten hearts. Five of them are inside hearts. Five of them are outside hearts. We'll put the inside hearts inside the paper bag. We'll put the outside hearts outside the paper bag.

Give each child the heart cards. Let the children cut out the heart cards and fill out the information. If you have non-readers in the group, you may want to pair them with someone who is a reader.

Provide a scale and a tape measure so that the children can fill in all the information. When all ten hearts are completed, put the inside hearts inside the bag. Tape or glue the outside hearts to the outside of the bag. Fold over the tops of the bags and staple. Write the children's names on the bottoms of the bags.

Set the bags in the center of a circle. Mix them up. Have the children sit on the floor.

Say: Let's use the outside part to see if we can tell whose bag is whose. If you know it is your bag, keep it a secret and see if we can place all the bags.

Read the different characteristics from the outside of the bags. Try to match the bags with their owners. When all the bags have a match, let the children decide if the matches are correct. Then let them swap until they get theirs.

When all the children have their bags, toss a ball to a child and invite him or her to share one of the "inside" hearts. Do not force any child to disclose these feelings.

Say: In today's story we learn that God not only sees our outside, but God also sees our insides. And God loves us just as we are.

God loves us just as we are.

Supplies

Reproducible 6B, paper lunch bags, scissors, pencils, crayons or felt-tip markers, tape or glue, scale, tape measure, staple and staples, ball

You're the One!

by LeeDell Stickler

Have the children sit in a circle of chairs.

Say: Today's Bible story is about a secret plan between Samuel the judge and God. There is excitement and plots and adventure. It wasn't easy to be God's servant. Sometimes you had to do things that put your life in danger.

As I tell the story of how David the shepherd boy became the king of Israel, I want you to participate. I want you to pretend that you are with Samuel as he sneaks out of the palace and makes his way to Bethlehem to find the new king. We have to be really sneaky because if King Saul finds out we're leaving, we're sure to lose our heads.

Have the children form a line, one behind the other, for the words and action section of the story. At the place indicated in the story, pause long enough for the children to form a line.

Words and Actions

Sneak, sneak, sneak
Out the city gates.
(Creep around the circle on tiptoe, trying not to make a noise.)
Sssh! Sssh! Sssh!
Don't say a single word.
(Put fingers to lips and turn first to the person in front of you and then behind you and shush them.)
Samuel's on a mission
To crown a brand new king.
(Come back to original places.)

One day God said, "Samuel,
the time has finally come.
The man that I put on the throne
His time as king is done.

"Saul chose to disobey me
Against your wise advice.
I'll teach that man a lesson.
He'll not do this twice.

I've looked at all my people
And found the one that's right.
You must go out to Bethlehem.
Leave this very night."

Words and Actions

Samuel paused a moment.
His heart filled up with fear.
"Just how am I to do this?
On this I'm not quite clear.

Suppose Saul should discover
Just what I am about.

Suppose the king should find
That I'm not in, but out?"

"You'll say you're off to Jesse's
house
To have a great big feast. No one
will know your purpose,
Not in the very least."

Words and Actions

When the elders of the city
Found that Samuel was on the way,
They knew that he brought trouble.
They'd prefer he didn't stay.

But when he got to Jesse's place
Samuel told them why he'd come.
"Bring forward each of your
strapping boys,
Send them here one by one."

Words and Actions

Each boy passed by old Samuel.
Samuel waited for a sign.
"Which one have you chosen,
God?
Shall I do it one more time?"

Words and Actions

"I do not see as others do.
They only see outside.
I know the hearts of people,
The part that lives inside."

I've one more son named David.
He is the youngest one.
He keeps a watch on all the sheep.
That's why he didn't come."

Words and Actions

He may be the chosen one
'Till he's here, we will not know.
He needs to be with all the rest.
Please bid a servant go."

David hurried from the hillside
As fast as he could come.
He stood before old Samuel,
And God said, "He's the one!"

I've looked into this shepherd boy.
I've seen what's in his heart.
He'll be the kind of king I wanted
For my people from the start.

Words and Actions

So Samuel took the horn of oil
And blessed the brand new king.
Soon David would sit on the throne.
Rejoice, give praise, and sing.

Words and Actions

Supplies

None

Who's the One?

Say: God knew who the new king would be. God knew David from the inside out. Let's see if we know one another that well.

Select one child to be "IT." Have IT leave the room or face the wall while you select one child to be the heart. Invite IT to turn back around.

Say: It is up to you to find out who's the one. You will ask the question to the whole group. The person who is the heart must go "thump, thump," just like a heart. Let's practice a couple of times.

Have IT ask the question and have the whole class make the thumping sound of a heart. Then have the children cup their hands over their mouths and stop thumping. When the game starts, only the child who has been selected makes the sound.

Every time IT asks, "Who's the one?" the person that the teacher selected has to answer "thump, thump." IT can ask this three times. If IT doesn't get it, IT has to do it again. If IT discovers who's the one, then the two will trade places.

Supplies

chairs

Body Boggled

This activity will be a fun way to learn the Bible verse. Have the children form a circle with their chairs. Select one person to be "IT." Remove IT's chair from the circle and close it back in.

Say: Today's Bible verse is, "The LORD looks on the heart." Let's say it together. *(Let the children practice.)* **Whenever the person in the center says, "The LORD looks on the heart," then everyone has to trade places. IT will be trying to get a chair.**

However, IT may try to fool you. If you leave your chair at the wrong word, you are automatically caught. Instead of saying, "The LORD looks on the heart," IT may use a different body part. For example, IT might say "The LORD looks on the kidney or the ankle, or the ear." But don't move unless you hear the word "heart."

Play until several children have had an opportunity to be IT or until the class begins to get bored.

Affirmations and Prayer

Have the children sit in a circle either in chairs or on the floor.

Say: Let's play a game. Start passing the ball around the circle as I sing our Bible verse. You can sing along with me once you learn the song. When I stop the singing, we will say something nice about whoever is holding the ball. We'll say something nice about this person on the outside and on the inside.

Start passing the ball as you sing "The Lord Looks on the Heart" to the tune of "The Farmer in the Dell."

The Lord Looks on the Heart
(Tune: "The Farmer in the Dell")

"The Lord looks on the heart.
The Lord looks on the heart."
It doesn't matter who you are,
"The Lord looks on the heart."

Stop and start singing so that all the children get a chance to be affirmed by the group. If you are uncomfortable singing with the children, use a CD of Christian music.

Ask: What did we learn about God from today's lesson? *(God loves us just as we are.)*

God loves us just as we are.

Say: God loves each and every one of us. Because God does love each of us, we are connected to one another not only because we all go to this church or attend this group, but also because we are part of God's family. Let's connect with each other for our prayer.

Have the children stand in a circle and hold hands.

Pray: Dear God, we are so glad that you see us the way we really area and still love us. We know that we are not always lovable, but we try. Help our insides to be as pretty as our outsides. Amen.

Supplies

ball, optional: CD and CD player

Reproducible 6A

My hair is ________.	________ makes me laugh.
My eyes are ________.	________ makes me cry.
I am ________ inches tall.	I can do ________ well.
I weigh ________ pounds.	I wish I could ________.
I look like ________.	What I like best about me is ________.

REPRODUCIBLE 6B

Lesson
7

All-in-One BIBLE FUN ELEMENTARY

David Plays the Harp

Bible Verse

Praise God with trumpets and all kinds of harps.

Psalm 150:3, CEV

Bible Story

1 Samuel 16:14–23

Once Saul fell out of favor with God, he was at the mercy of his own ungovernable temperament. The Scriptures speak of an "evil spirit" or "evil force;" we see it as a depression. When he was in a deeply depressed state, he was not able to rule the kingdom.

His servants, searching for a way to comfort him, suggested the therapeutic value of music, and someone mentioned David to Saul. Saul sent for David, who arrived bearing gifts from his father, Jesse, and the first meeting between the current king and the man that God had chosen to replace him took place. David's musical therapy was successful and Saul took an instant liking to David, even making him his personal military aide. Probably at this point neither of them had any idea what was in store. As Saul's downward spiral was beginning, so was David's upward journey. It is good to remember that although God had rejected Saul as king because of Saul's rebellion, God still sent the remedy for Saul's melancholia through music.

David played a lyre, a four-stringed harp shaped like a flat box, with two arms joined by a crosspiece. David had spent many nights alone in the hills caring for his father's sheep. When the sheep were settled for the night, David sat on the hillside, playing his harp and singing his praises to God.

Scientists in brain research have learned that music is a powerful teaching tool. It can be a stimulant or a relaxer. Music can act as a vehicle for words, images, and concepts. Music also primes the neural pathways for future learning. God had indeed given David a powerful gift to use, and he was called to use it to help King Saul.

God also gives us gifts that we can use to help others. Children enjoy helping. Affirm their contributions. Give them many opportunities to help others, either directly or indirectly. This affirms them as treasured children of God.

We can use our talents to help others feel better.

If time is limited, we recommend those activities that are noted in **boldface**. Depending on your time and the number of children, you may be able to include more activities.

Activity	Time	Supplies
Music Boxes	10 minutes	boxes and box lids, plain paper, tape, crayons or felt-tip markers, rubber bands
Musical Drawing	**10 minutes**	**paper, crayons or felt-tip markers, optional: CD and CD player**
Feelings	10 minutes	Bible; Reproducible 7A; crayons, colored pencils, or felt-tip markers
Bible Story: "David Plays for King Saul: A Musical"	**10 minutes**	**None**
Praise God With Trumpets!	10 minutes	Reproducible 7B, crayons or felt-tip markers, tape or glue, scissors
Toot Your Own Horn	5 minutes	paper trumpets
Talented Help	10 minutes	ball
Thumbody Special Prayers	**5 minutes**	**None**

Music Boxes

Supplies

boxes and box lids, plain paper, tape, crayons or felt-tip markers, rubber bands

Provide a variety of boxes and box lids such as shoe box lids or boxes that greeting cards or blank checks come in.

If the boxes have writing on the outside, help the children wrap the boxes and box lids in plain paper. Encourage the children to decorate the boxes with crayons or felt-tip markers.

Show the children how to stretch rubber bands around the lids or open boxes, placing the bands at least half an inch apart.

Show the children how to use their thumbs and index fingers to pluck the rubber bands. To get a variety of sounds, each box should have both thick and thin rubber bands.

Say: We are turning these boxes into a Bible-times musical instrument known as a lyre. Modern-day harps are payed the same way as lyres were once played, by plucking the strings. David played a lyre as he watched his sheep. God gave David musical talent. He became an excellent musician on the lyre. In today's Bible story we will hear how David used his talent to help others.

We can use our talents to help others feel better.

Musical Drawing

Supplies

paper, crayons or felt-tip markers, optional: CD and CD player

Give each child a piece of paper. Have the children fold the paper in half and then fold it in half again. When they open their papers, they should have four equal quadrants. Place different colors of crayons or markers on the table so that the children can easily reach them as you change songs.

Say: David's music made King Saul feel better. I'm going to sing to you. When you hear the song, I want you to draw the way the music makes you feel. I'll sing four different songs, so use one square of your paper to draw during each separate piece. You don't have to draw pictures but you can choose colors and lines to show how the music makes you feel.

Sing "God Is So Good," "If You're Happy and You Know It," "Jesus Loves Me," and "I've Been Working on the Railroad." Encourage the children to draw how the music makes them feel. (If you are uncomfortable singing for the children, choose different kinds of music from a Christian music CD.)

Feelings

Supplies

Bible; Reproducible 7A; crayons, colored pencils, or felt-tip markers

Photocopy the feelings page **(Reproducible 7A)** for each child.

Say: Today our Bible story is about David and King Saul. David had a special talent. He sang and played the harp. He often played the harp to keep the sheep calm when they were on the hillside. He also wrote songs. Many of the songs David wrote are in a special song book.

Ask: Can you guess where we find this song book? *(The Bible)*

Say: It is a book in our Bible, the Book of Psalms.

Show the children where the Book of Psalms is located in the Bible. *(It is in the center of the Bible.)*

Give each child the feelings page.

Say: David and the other people who wrote these psalms showed their feelings with their words. Listen as I read the parts of several psalms. Then tell me how you think the person who wrote them was feeling. Once we've decided what feeling the psalm expresses, find the box with that feeling on your paper. Then draw a face inside the box that shows that feeling.

Read the following verses:

Psalm 137:1 *(sad)*
Psalm 47:1 *(happy)*
Psalm 3:1 *(afraid)*
Psalm 9:1 *(thankful)*

Say: In our Bible story today King Saul is feeling angry and sad. David uses his talent to play the harp for Saul. The music calms the king and makes him feel better.

We can use our talents to help others feel better.

Ask: What are some things you can do to help others feel better? *(make them a get-well card, give someone a hug, be quiet while someone is resting, smile, and so forth)*

David Plays for the King
A Musical

by LeeDell Stickler, Lisa Flinn, and Barbara Younger

In this musical play, you will read the parts of King Saul and his servants. To make your parts sound musical, chant your lines in a sing-song style. To create the chorus, divide the children into two groups. The first group will become the "Worry Chorus." The second group will be the "Harp Chorus." Both groups will sing their words to the tune of "The Farmer in the Dell."

Practice singing these choruses with the groups. Tell the children you will point to each group when it is their turn to sing.

King Saul: Aw, oh, ugh. I feel terrible!

Worry Chorus:
King Saul is feeling bad.
King Saul is feeling bad.
O my! What can we do?
King Saul is feeling bad.

King Saul: In fact, I feel so horrible that it scares me. Something is wrong. I'm worried!

Servants: King Saul, you are not yourself. Let us help you.

King Saul: How can you help? How can anyone possibly help?

Worry Chorus:
King Saul is feeling bad.
King Saul is feeling bad.
O my! What can we do?
King Saul is feeling bad.

Servants: Perhaps if someone were to play quiet, soothing music, you would feel better.

King Saul: Quiet, soothing music? You mean like on a harp. I'd like that.

Worry Chorus:
King Saul is feeling bad.
King Saul is feeling bad.
O my! What can we do?
King Saul is feeling bad.

Servants: We know someone who is very good at playing the harp.

King Saul: He must be very talented. I don't want any wrong notes or loud music.

Servants: This one is special. Not only does he play the harp well, but he is also brave and strong. He doesn't talk too much and God is with him. His father is Jesse from Bethlehem.

King Saul: Send for him at once. I cannot go on like this much longer. This feeling inside me is just too terrible to bear!

Servants: We will send for him at once.

Worry Chorus:
King Saul is feeling bad.
King Saul is feeling bad.
O my! What can we do?
King Saul is feeling bad.

Servants: David is here with his harp and other gifts for you.

King Saul: Finally! Bring David and his harp to me right now.

Harp Chorus:
O David played the harp.
O David played the harp.
David played to help the King.
O David played the harp.

King Saul: What a relief! I'm feeling better already.

Harp Chorus:
O David played the harp.
O David played the harp.
David played to help the King.
O David played the harp.

King Saul: David, your music is really helping me. I want you to stay with me.

Servants: As you wish, King Saul.

King Saul: More music!

Harp Chorus:
O David played the harp.
O David played the harp.
David played to help the King.
O David played the harp.

Supplies

Reproducible 7B, crayons or felt-tip markers, tape or glue, scissors

Praise God With Trumpets

Photocopy the trumpet **(Reproducible 7B)** for each child.

Say: Our Bible verse for today tells us to "Praise God with trumpets and all kinds of harps" (Psalm 150:3, CEV). David praised God with a harp. Now, let us praise God with trumpets .

Give each child a trumpet. Invite the children to decorate their trumpets and cut them out. Help the children tape the seams of the trumpets together.

Have the children bring their trumpets and form a line behind you. Have everyone sing "toot-toot" through their trumpets. Then tell the children to repeat after you, one line at a time, as you "toot-toot" the tune to "Praise God from Whom All Blessings Flow." Finally, march around the room tooting this tune.

Ask: Does anyone remember any of the words to the song we just played?

Say: It is the Doxology. It is the song we use to praise God. We can praise God with singing, with harps and trumpets, and with other musical instruments.

Say the Bible verse together with the children. Repeat the verse by saying it through the trumpets as you and the children march around the room one more time.

Supplies

paper trumpets

Toot Your Own Horn

Have the children bring their horns made in the "Praise God With Trumpets" activity and sit down in an open area of the room. Stand across the space from the children.

Say: God gave David the talent to play the harp, sing songs, and write music. Then David used that talent to help King Saul feel better. God gives each one of us our own special talents. Let's think about our own talents. I will name some talents. If it is a talent God has given you, jump up, run up here next to me, and toot your own horn.

Name the talents listed below. You may want to add others specific to your group of children. Make sure you name at least one talent for each child.

dancing	sports	writing	running
fishing	ice skating	skate boarding	roller skating
gymnastics	drawing	cooking	sewing
speaking	math	building	using a computer
reading	smiling	singing	playing instruments
being a leader	jumping	swimming	remembering

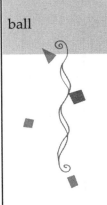

Talented Help

Supplies

ball

Have the children stand in a circle.

Say: God gave David the talent to sing, play the harp, and write songs. God gives each of us our own talents. Your talent might be playing a musical instrument like David, it might be drawing, dancing, playing sports, or reading. I'm going to bounce the ball to someone in our circle. Whoever catches the ball will tell us one of his or her talents. Then bounce the ball back to me.

Bounce the ball to a child in the circle. Encourage the child who catches the ball to name a talent and then bounce the ball back to you. Continue until every child has an opportunity to catch the ball.

Say: You are very talented! Now let's think about how we can use our talents to help others feel better. This time when I bounce the ball to you, name a way you might use your talent to help someone feel better. For instance, if your talent is drawing you can make get-well cards. If your talent is playing sports you could invite someone to play with you or watch a game you are playing.

Bounce the ball around the circle again and encourage the children to answer.

Thumbody Special Prayers

Supplies

None

Have the children stand in a circle and extend their right hands—thumb extended to the left and the fingers folded over. Each child will enclose the thumb of the person to their right inside their folded fingers, forming a circle.

Say: One way we can help others feel better is by praying for them. Is there anyone you want to pray for today?

Encourage the children to tell you any prayer requests. Then include those requests and the beginning or end of your prayer.

Pray: Dear God, you have made each one of us somebody special. Thank you for giving each one of us our own talents. Help us be like David and use our talents to help others feel better. Amen.

We can use our talents to help others feel better.

Happy	Sad
Thankful	Afraid

REPRODUCIBLE 7A

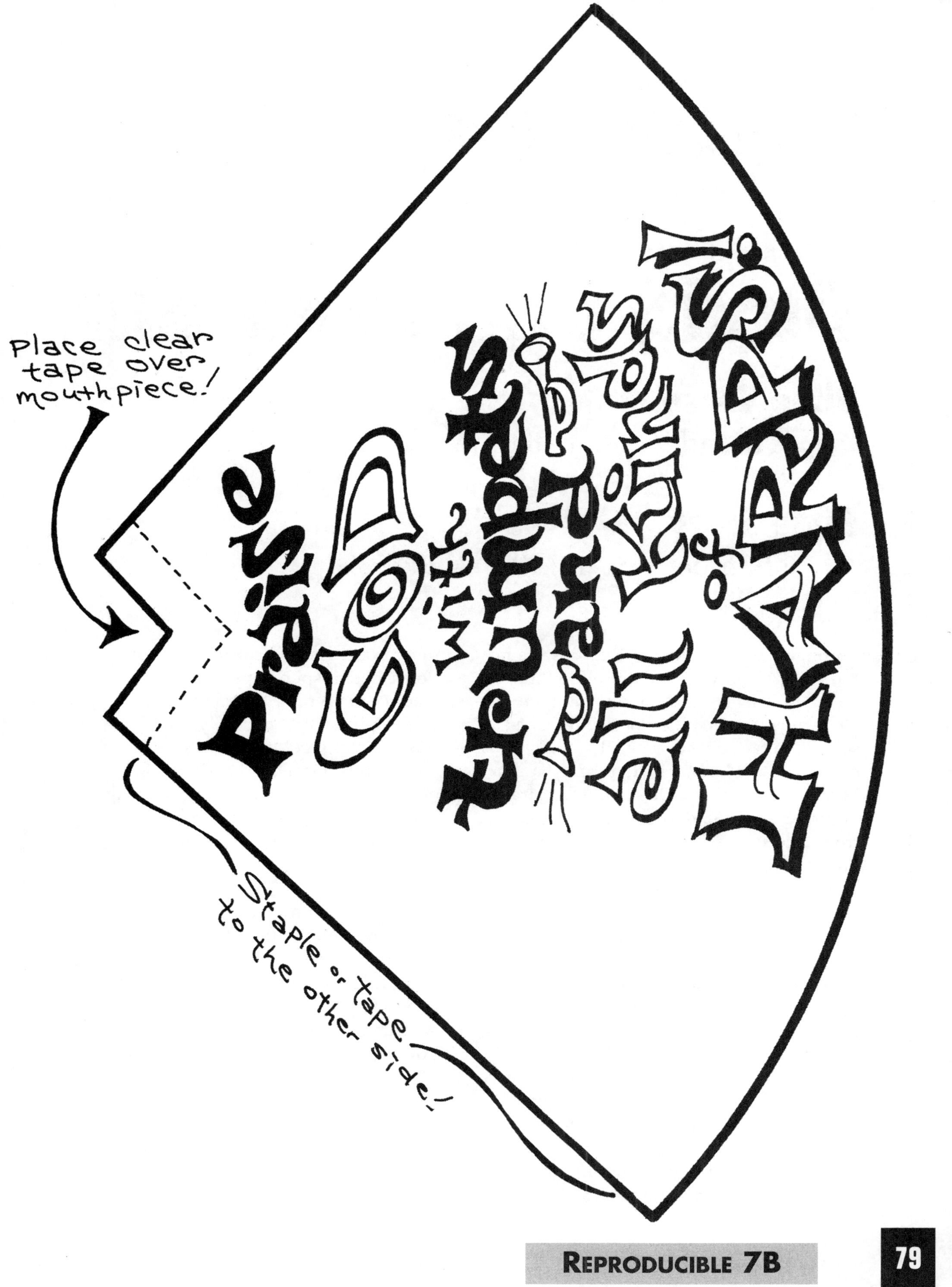
Place clear tape over mouthpiece!
Praise God with trumpets and all sounds of HARPS!
Staple or tape to the other side!

David and Jonathan

Bible Verse

A friend loves at all times.

Proverbs 17:17

Bible Story

1 Samuel 18:1–16; 19:1–7; 20:1–42

Through a variety of circumstances, David the shepherd boy found himself in the palace of King Saul. He became not only the court musician but also an accomplished soldier. In fact, he was so well liked by everyone who knew him that King Saul became very jealous. One of the last straws occurred when Saul and his armies returned from a decisive battle, and David received greater praise than the king himself.

During this time at the palace, David had formed a close friendship with Jonathan, King Saul's son. The two boys are held up as the epitome of what it means to be a friend. Jonathan even risked going against his father to save his friend's life. David and Jonathan's covenant of friendship is reminiscent of God's covenant with human beings. This promise reminds us of the covenant between people and God.

In some ways holding up the story of David and Jonathan as an example is a bit dangerous. The two boys' friendship flourished in spite of parental disapproval. Had it not been for the fact that Saul was a mean spirited and mentally unstable man, this might not be the best of stories to use as an example. But David and Jonathan exhibited the true nature of friendship—the ability to stand up for one another and to be there for one another at all times—in spite of trouble.

Elementary children are beginning to look more and more to their friends for affirmation and approval. Peer pressure is becoming a significant influence in their lives. Help them to steer away from destructive relationships. Encourage, however, the outreach to others.

Elementary can begin to understand that God is our friend, too. God loves us just the way we are. God forgives us when we do wrong. God listens. God is always there for us.

Friends love one another.

If time is limited, we recommend those activities that are noted in **boldface**. Depending on your time and the number of children, you may be able to include more activities.

Activity	Time	Supplies	
Friendship Finds	**5 minutes**	**Reproducible 8A, masking tape, scissors, basket**	Join the Fun
Minefield Mania	10 minutes	yarn, blindfolds,unbreakable items from your room such as a chair, a book, a pillow, and a box of crayons	
Set the Stage	5 minutes	newspaper	Bible Story Fun
Bible Story: Friends Forever	**10 minutes**	**newspaper balls**	
Balloon Sandwich	10 minutes	masking tape or yarn, balloons	
Celebrate Friends	10 minutes	Reproducible 8B, crayons or felt-tip markers, scissors, pencil, construction paper, white glue, large piece of paper	
Friendship Stretch	5 minutes	None	Live the Fun
Prayer Partners	**5 minutes**	**None**	

Supplies

Reproducible 8A, masking tape, scissors, basket

Friendship Finds

Make a copy of the friendship finds **(Reproducible 8A)**. If you have more than twelve children, make two copies of the pictures and add as many pairs as you need. Cut the cards apart and put them in a basket. As the children enter the room, attach a friendship find to the front of their shirt or dress with masking tape.

Say: Some things just go together naturally, like peanut butter and jelly and ice cream and cake. Some friends go together so well that you don't think of one without thinking of the other. Each of you is wearing a friendship find. When I say "go," I want you to look around the room and find your matching friend. When you find your friend, sit down together. This friend will be your partner for the next few activities.

Say: Today's Bible story is about one of the greatest friendships of all times, David and Jonathan. In today's Bible story we learn that a friend loves at all times.

Friends love one another.

Supplies

yarn, blindfolds,unbreakable items from your room such as a chair, a book, a pillow, and a box of crayons

Minefield Mania

Say: Friends also help one another. Let's play a game where one friend will help another get through a dangerous minefield. One of the friends will be blindfolded. The other friend will use verbal clues to guide the second friend safely through the minefield.

Make a circle with a twenty-foot-long piece of yarn. Inside the yarn arrange several items from your classroom. Make sure the items are unbreakable.

Then let the pairs decide who is going to be the crawler and who is going to be the guide. Place the blindfold on the crawler.

When the crawler gets from one side of the circle to the other, the crawler becomes the guide and the guide the crawler. If a crawler bumps into an object, he or she must leave the minefield and get in line to try again.

Make sure the children have an opportunity to be both. If you have a large class, create more than one circle so that several teams can play at the same time.

Set the Stage

Give each child several sheets of newspaper. Have the children wad the newspaper into balls and place the balls beneath their chairs.

Say: In today's Bible story you will play an important part. First, you are going to be King Saul when he gets angry. When King Saul gets angry, he throws things. But instead of throwing dangerous things, you will be throwing newspaper balls. You will hear your part in the story. One of you will also be David and play the harp.

Second, whenever you hear David's name, stand up and do the "cabbage patch." Put your fists together in front of you, your arms forming a circle. Circle your arms to the right while you circle your hips to the left.

Third, at certain places in the story you will sign the Bible verse.

Teach the children words from American Sign Language for the verse. Because American Sign Language does not translate literally, the verse will actually says friends love all the time.

Supplies

newspaper

Friends
love
all
the time
Hook the right index over the left which is palm-up and repeat in reverse
Open hands are crossed at the wrist and are pressed to the heart
The left open hand faces the body~ Make a circle with the right hand going out and around the left hand, ending up with the back of the right hand in the palm of the left.
Crook the index finger and tap the back of the left hand several times as though pointing to a watch.

Friends Forever

by LeeDell Stickler

Follow the directions in "Set the Stage" (page 83) to involve the children in this story.

King Saul felt angry. He didn't know why he was angry. All he knew was that he was angry. And when he was angry he did angry things—like throwing things at people. So he did.
(Everyone throws newspaper balls.)

"Music will make you feel better," suggested a servant. "You need someone who can play soothing music when you are feeling angry."

"Not a bad idea," thought King Saul. "Do you know someone?"

"I have heard that Jesse's youngest son plays the harp and sings. He is a fine young man, and the Lord is with him," said the servant.

"Send for him immediately," said King Saul. *(Throw newspaper balls at the wall.)* "If the Lord is with him, then maybe the Lord will be with me again." So they sent word to Jesse, and **David**, the shepherd boy and harp player, came to the palace to live.

Everyone liked **David**. He was a loyal servant and a good leader. Saul came to love him as much as he loved his son Jonathan. In fact, Jonathan and **David** soon became best friends. They were always together, just like real brothers.

One day **David** said, "Jonathan, we will always be friends." *(Sign the Bible verse.)*

"Yes," said Jonathan. "Let's make a promise today that no matter what happens, we'll always be friends." The two clasped hands. *(Sign the Bible verse.)*

Because **David** was so well liked, King Saul appointed him as the leader of the army. **David** became such a good soldier that soon the people loved **David** more than King Saul. This made the king very angry.

Then while **David** was playing the harp and singing for the king, King Saul began to think. The more he thought, the the angrier he became. "What if the people decided to make **David** king instead of me? I wouldn't like that a bit." King Saul picked up his spear and threw it at the harp player. *(Sign the Bible verse.)*

Fortunately **David** was very quick, and he ducked. The spear stuck in the wall just above his head.

Jonathan was worried about his father's feelings toward his friend. "For some reason my father is angry with you. It is not safe for you at the palace. Go hide until I can find out what's going on." *(Sign the Bible verse.)*

David could not think of anything that he had done wrong. But he knew the king was trying to kill him. So he ran away from the palace. Jonathan and he invented a secret code. Jonathan wanted to protect his friend. But first, Jonathan had to talk with his father. *(Sign the Bible verse.)*

King Saul was not himself. Even though he promised his son that he would not try to harm **David**, Jonathan knew better. Jonathan was sure that if the harp player returned to the palace his father would kill him. *(Sign the Bible verse.)*

The next day Jonathan went out to the field. He took his servant with him. Jonathan drew back his bow and launched an arrow into the air. "Run and fetch the arrow," said Jonathan. The servant began running and stopped beside the arrow. But Jonathan said, "Look, the arrow is beyond you. Hurry. Do not linger." *(Sign the Bible verse.)*

The servant was confused. He was holding the arrow. How could it be beyond him? But this was the secret signal that **David** and Jonathan had decided upon. Jonathan was telling his friend to leave immediately and not to return. *(Sign the Bible verse.)*

Jonathan sent his servant back to the palace so he and **David** could see each other one last time. **David** came out from his hiding place. The two friends hugged each another. "Go in peace," said Jonathan. "May God be with both of us and with all our descendants forever." *(Sign the Bible verse.)*

Balloon Sandwich

Supplies

masking tape or yarn, balloons

Say: David and Jonathan were great friends. Jonathan was ready to risk his position as prince to protect his friend David. He was even willing to risk his life. Now let's play a game where friends help one another.

Blow up a balloon for each pair of friends. Mark a beginning line and an ending line with either masking tape or yarn. Have the children hold the balloon between them back to back. The friends must move from a starting point to an ending point while holding the balloon between their backs. If the balloon falls down, then they start again.

Say: Today we have learned that friends love one another. When friends love one another that means they care, they share, they help, they look out for, and they show appreciation for one another.

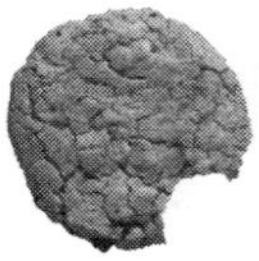

Friends love one another.

Celebrate Friends

Supplies

Reproducible 8B, crayons or felt-tip markers, scissors, pencil, construction paper, white glue, large piece of paper

Photocopy the friendship cards **(Reproducible 8B)**. Make enough copies so that the children can have as many as they need.

Ask: What are some of the things that friends do for one another?

Make a list of those things on a large piece of paper. You may need to suggest some things to help the children start on their list. Suggest things like play together, celebrate one another's birthdays, help one another with homework, share snacks, and so forth. If a child does not mention prayer, be sure to add pray for one another to the list.

Say: One nice thing we can do for our friends is to tell them how special they are to us. Let's make friendship cards that we can give to our friends that say "thank you" for being such a good friends.

Give each child a piece of construction paper. Fold the construction paper in half and glue the friendship card on the outside. Let the children color the design and write their own messages on the insides of the cards.

Friendship Stretch

Supplies

None

Have the partners that were formed at the beginning of the lesson sit on the floor facing each another. Have them spread their legs into a V, feet touching. Have them grab hands. Then have one person lean back and pull the person opposite forward.

Say: Let's do a friendship stretch and say the Bible verse at the same time. Each of you will take turns saying a word as you lean back. As the other person leans back, he or she will say the second word of the verse and so on until the Bible verse is finished.

Remind the children of the Bible verse: "A friend loves at all times" (Proverbs 17:17). After the children have worked their way through the Bible verse several times, have them release hands.

Say: Friendship is sometimes pulling and sometimes giving. Friends are a special gift from God. Friends don't always get along. Friends don't always like exactly the same things. But friends do one thing. Friends always love one another.

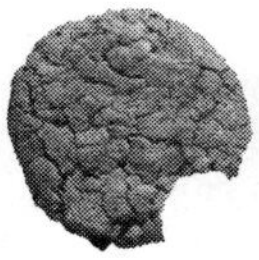

Friends love one another.

Prayer Partners

Supplies

None

Sing the song printed below to the tune of "She'll Be Coming 'Round the Mountain."

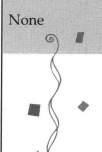

O, the Bible says a friend loves at all times.
O, the Bible says a friend loves at all times.
Just like Jonathan and David,
Just like Jonathan and David
O, the Bible says a friend loves at all times.

Say: Friends also pray for one another. This week I want you and your special friend for today to be prayer partners. Each night you will include your special friend in your prayer.

Have the children form a friendship circle.

Pray: Dear God, we thank you for our friends. Help us to love and share and help and care about them. Amen.

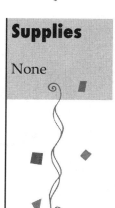

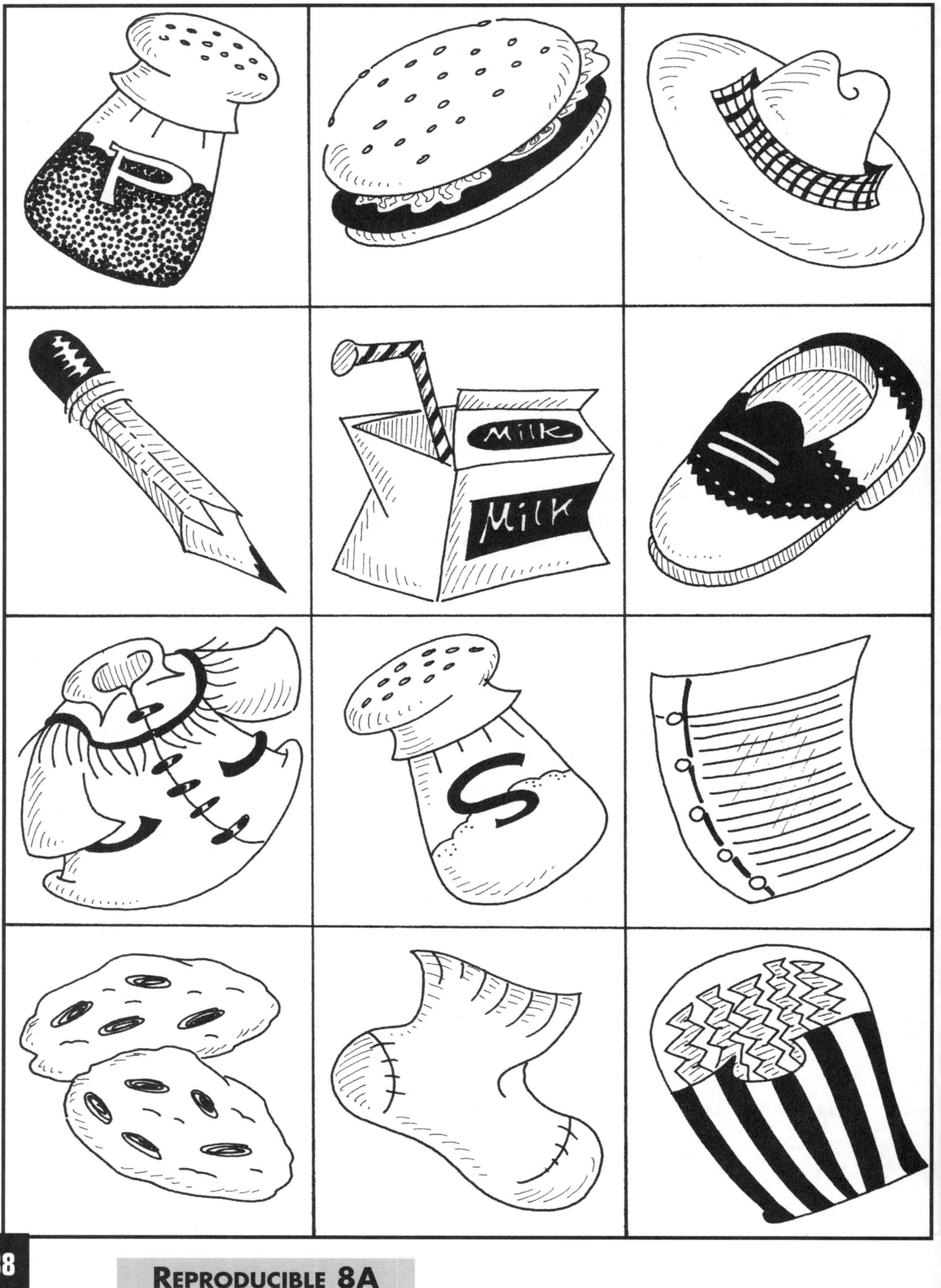

REPRODUCIBLE 8A

I'm glad you are my friend!

I'm glad you are my friend!

The Two Houses

Bible Verse

You shall love the Lord your God with all your heart.
Luke 10:27

Bible Story

Luke 6:46-49; Matthew 7:24-27

A parable is a story that makes a single point and needs very little explanation to make its meaning clear. Jesus used parables about common, everyday objects and situations to help the people understand what he was trying to tell them. Frequently Jesus compared theological and moral teachings with familiar happenings in his listeners' lives or surroundings.

The story of the house on the rock is a parable that tells both what something is like and also what it is not like. The illustration of the two houses must have occurred naturally to Jesus, who probably had been a carpenter. His listeners would have understood the reference to building on sand because in the topography of their country sand often was found in wadis, the dry beds of seasonal rivers. During the dry season one might safely and easily build a house in a wadi. But with the coming of the rainy season, water would gush down the wadi and carry such a house away because it had no foundation.

Jesus was making the point that persons who understood his words and lived according to them were building their lives on a strong foundation of faith and love. Those who seemed to listen and understand but did not live accordingly would not have strong inner reserves to call on when adversity came.

Jesus' story talked about a foundation of faith and love, both very abstract concepts. Although elementary children are still concrete thinkers, they can appreciate why one house stood firm and the other did not. A few may be able to make the connection that Jesus really was talking about building one's faith and one's life on a strong foundation of love and trust in him and in God. Help the boys and girls you teach understand how they feel when they are sitting and standing on a firm base. You can help them begin to understand that loving God and Jesus is to have a strong base on which to stand, sit, and grow.

We can listen to God's Word and learn from it.

If time is limited, we recommend those activities that are noted in **boldface**. Depending on your time and the number of children, you may be able to include more activities.

Activity	Time	Supplies
Crazy Construction	**10 minutes**	**2 decks of playing cards, 2 boxes of toothpicks, resealable plastic bags, 2 bath towels, newspaper, modeling clay**
Flood Alert!	10 minutes	masking tape or chairs
Wicked Washout!	5 minutes	Reproducible 9B, two aluminum cookie sheets (with sides), sand (slightly damp), rocks, two plastic containers, plastic cup, water, resealable plastic bags
Sing the Bible Story	5 minutes	None
Bible Story: The House on the Rocks	**10 minutes**	**puppet**
Foundation Station	10 minutes	large mural paper, tempera paint, newspaper, paper towels, paper plates, smocks, masking tape, paint brushes, felt-tip markers
Flip Out!	10 minutes	Reproducibles 9A and B, crayons or markers, stapler, scissors, construction paper
Balloon Frenzy	5 minutes	permanent felt-tip marker, balloons, optional: CD of Christian music and CD player
Parable Prayers	**10 minutes**	**a rock**

Crazy Construction

Supplies

2 decks of playing cards, 2 boxes of toothpicks, resealable plastic bags, 2 bath towels, newspaper, modeling clay

Before the children arrive, set out four activity tables (three to four children per table). On two of the tables put a bath towel and a deck of playing cards. On the other two tables put newspaper, a box of toothpicks, and several sticks of modeling clay.

Greet the children as they arrive. Assign the children to the tables and let them begin building.

Say: Today we are going to learn about building. I want each team to build a structure. At the end of five minutes the table with the tallest structure wins. Those working with a deck of cards will have to balance the cards on one another. Those working with toothpicks will use small balls of modeling clay to attach one toothpick to another.

After five minutes tell everyone to stop.

Ask: Which buildings were the tallest? *(The ones built with toothpicks and modeling clay should be the tallest.)* **Why?** *(because they were sturdier)* **What would happen if I blew on or tapped each structure?** *(Tap each structure. The houses of cards should fall over. The ones with the toothpicks should continue to stand.)* **What makes the difference?** *(The toothpicks have a stronger foundation.)*

Flood Alert!

Supplies

masking tape or chairs

Say: In Bible times flooding was something that happened all the time. So people knew you had to be careful when it rained. You also had to be careful where you built your house. Flash floods could be very dangerous. Let's play a game called "Flood Alert!". The object will be to get to safe ground before the Flood comes. I will choose someone to be "IT." IT will warn people. The area marked around IT will be the flood zone. The object is to get through the flood zone to the safe zone without being trapped by the water.

Use masking tape or chairs to identify three different areas. Mark a safe zone at one end of the room. Ten feet out from the safe zone will be the flood zone. On the other side of the flood zone are the townspeople.

IT will face away from the group. The group will stand behind the flood zone. When IT says "now," the townspeople will try to get through the flood zone to the safe zone. If IT turns around and shouts out "Flood Alert!" the persons who are caught in the flood zone are drowned and must sit down. Play several times until several children get to be IT.

Wicked Washout!

Supplies

Reproducible 9B, two aluminum cookie sheets (with sides), sand (slightly damp), rocks, two plastic containers, plastic cup, water, resealable plastic bags

Make two copies of the house **(Reproducible 9B)**. Then assemble the two houses.

Put sand and rocks in separate plastic containers. Put the water in a cup. In a resealable bag punch several holes so you can simulate rain.

Have the children gather around a table. Place the two cookie sheets in the center of the table. In the center of one sheet empty the container of slightly damp sand. In the center of the other sheet empty the container of rocks. Pile the sand in the center of the sheet. Do the same for the rocks.

Say: Once upon a time there were two men who decided to build houses. The first man thought, "I'm going to build my house here. *(Place the house on the sand mound.)* **It is close to water, and it will be easy to build." The second man thought, "I'm going to build my house here.** *(Place the house on the rock mound.)* **It won't be easy to build, but I think it will be stronger."**

Ask: What do you think happened when the rains came? *(Let the children guess what is going to happen.)*

Then choose one child to hold the plastic bag with holes in it over the house on the sand. Pour the water from the glass into the bag with holes. Watch what happens when it rains. Then do the same with the house on the rocks.

Ask: What do you learn from this story? *(Don't build on sand, pick a strong foundation)*

Say: Jesus used stories such as this to teach the people important lessons.

Sing the Bible Story

Supplies

None

Sing the song printed below to the tune of "She'll Be Coming 'Round the Mountain."

Now then if you build your house upon the sand.
Now then if you build your house upon the sand.
And the rains come splashing do-wn,
And the rains come splashing do-wn.
You will find your house will no longer stand.

Now then if you build your house upon hard ground.
Now then if you build your house upon hard ground.
And the rains come splashing do-wn,
And the rains come splashing do-wn.
You will find your house forever stands.

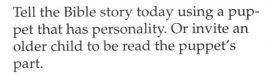

The House on the Rocks

by LeeDell Stickler

Tell the Bible story today using a puppet that has personality. Or invite an older child to be read the puppet's part. Or if there is a child in your group who is a confident reader, let him or her play the role. If you are planning this lesson ahead of time, make a copy of the script and let the child take it home to practice.

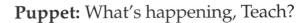

Puppet: What's happening, Teach?

Teach: Not much, what's up with you?

Puppet: I just heard the funniest story.

Teach: Funny? Do you mean funny ha ha or funny strange?

Puppet: Both, actually. Jesus told a story about these two men who built houses.

Teach: There's nothing funny about building houses. People do it all the time.

Puppet: That's not what I meant. It was about where they built the houses that was funny.

Teach: Funny ha ha or funny strange?

Puppet: *(sighs)* Funny strange.

Teach: So, like, what happened?

Puppet: Well, one guy built his house on sand. Now, let's get real. What's going to happen to this house when it rains? I've been to the beach. I've built sand castles. I know what happens when those waves come in.

Teach: What happens?

Puppet: Swoosh! Flat, flat, flat, like a pancake. No one in his right mind would build a house on the sand.

Teach: What about the other guy?

Puppet: Now, he used his old noggin. He built his house on the rocks.

Teach: So that's a good thing?

Puppet: Right. When it rained, do you know what happened?

Teach: What?

Puppet: Absolutely nothing! Zippo! The rains fell down, and the house stood firm. Period. The end.

Teach: So, why did you find this story funny?

Puppet: Funny strange, not ha ha. You see, Jesus is always telling stories about God. Now, I listened real close to this story, but I couldn't figure out what it had to do with God. I mean, this story is about construction, not God.

Teach: Think about it a minute. Sometimes Jesus told stories about ordinary things to get people to think about God in a special way. What do you think the house built on the sand stands for?

Puppet: Well, it's not a very good house. The people who lived there would probably pray that it wouldn't rain a lot 'cause they know what's going to happen.

Teach: Now think about the house on the rocks. What does that make you think of?

Puppet: Hmm. Rocks, strong, hard, forever. Isn't there a Bible verse somewhere that talks about God being a rock? So if we think of that house being our belief in God, then Jesus is telling us we need a strong foundation. If we have a strong foundation, when bad times come, our house will stand firm and won't wash away. How's that!

Teach: Give me five!

Foundation Station

Supplies

large mural paper, tempera paint, newspaper, paper towels, paper plates, smocks, sponges, masking tape, paint brushes, felt-tip markers

Ask: What was the lesson that Jesus wanted the people who heard this story to know? *(That we need build a strong faith foundation.)*

Ask: How do we know how to build a strong foundation? *(We can read the Bible. Listen to our teachers. Listen to the pastor. Pray.)*

Say: When we read the Bible, we learn about God and about Jesus. We read what Jesus did and said. These things will help us to have a strong faith.

We can listen to God's Word and learn from it.

Cover the work area with newspaper and have the children wear paint smocks to protect their clothing. Make a paint pad by folding paper towels and placing them on paper plates. Pour tempera paint onto the paper towels. Tape the mural paper on the wall. Cut the sponges into square shapes.

Encourage the children to paint gray rocks at the bottom of the paper. Let the children use the square-shaped sponges to make flat-roofed Bible-times houses. Let the children take turns pressing the sponges onto the paint pad and then onto the mural paper on the rocks.

When each child has created a house, encourage him or her to use felt-tip markers to write something above that house that he or she has learned from the Bible.

Flip Out!

Supplies

Reproducibles 9A and B, crayons or markers, stapler, scissors, construction paper

Give each child a set of flip out cards (**Reproducibles 9A and 9B**).

Say: This is a fun way to remember the story of the wise man and the foolish man. Cut apart the cards. Then use one card as a pattern to cut a front and back from colored construction paper. Put the cards in order, beginning with the card labeled as number one on the bottom. Staple the cards at the top. Then flip the book and watch what happens to the two houses when the rain comes down.

If you have time, let the children make their own flip books of the story.

Balloon Frenzy

Supplies

permanent felt-tip marker, balloons, optional: CD of Chrisitan music and CD player

Before class, blow up enough balloons for each child in your class (but at least eleven). On the outside of eleven of the balloons use a permanent felt-tip marker to write one of the words from the Bible verse.

Bring the children to together in a circle. Give each child a balloon (some children may have a couple).

Say: Loving God with all your heart is one way to build a strong foundation. As I sing, you will keep the balloons in the air. When I stop singing, take the closest balloon to you. If it has a word on it, then you will hurry to put the Bible verse in order.

Go over the Bible verse so that the children are familiar with it: "You shall love the Lord your God with all your heart" (Luke 10:27).

Sing the song on page 93 for the children. Stop singing (in different places each time) to have the children put the Bible verse in order. If you are uncomfortable singing with the children use a CD of Christian music.

Parable Prayers

Supplies

a rock

Have the children sit in a circle.

Say: Jesus told stories called parables to help the people know more about God, what God was like, and what God expected from us.

Ask: What did we learn about God today? *(We can listen to God's word and learn from it.)* **Where do we hear God's word?** *(in the Bible)*

Show the children the rock.

Say: In today's parable the wise man built his house on a rock. Jesus wanted the people who heard this story to know that we need build a strong faith foundation. As we pass the rock around the circle, I want each of you to share something you do to build a strong faith foundation.

Pass the rock around the group. Do not force any child to contribute. When the rock has come all the way around the circle, set it in the center of the circle and have the children join hands.

Pray: Thank you, God, for the stories Jesus told. Help us to learn from them just as the people did long ago. Help us to listen to your word and to learn from it. Amen.

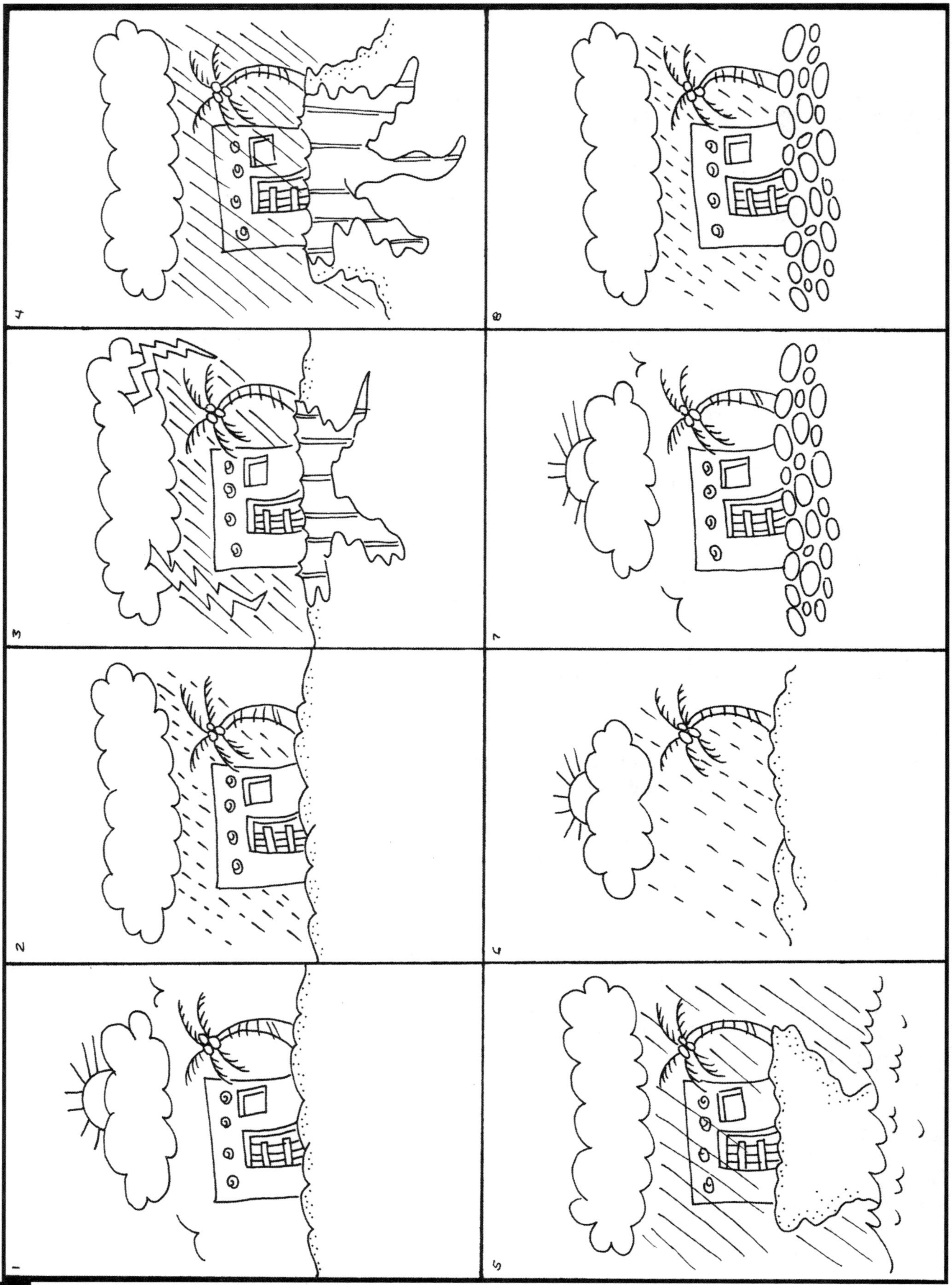

REPRODUCIBLE 9A

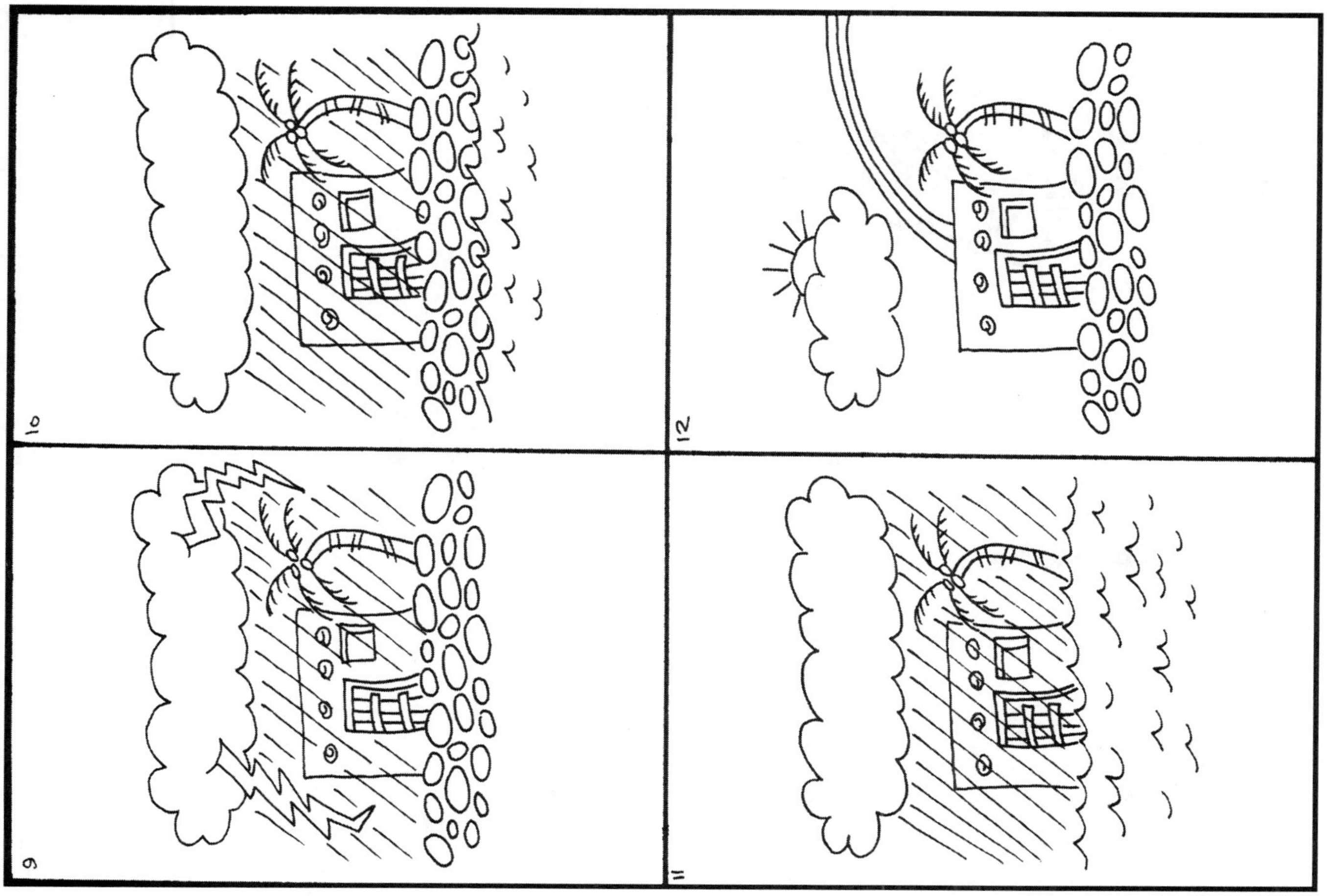

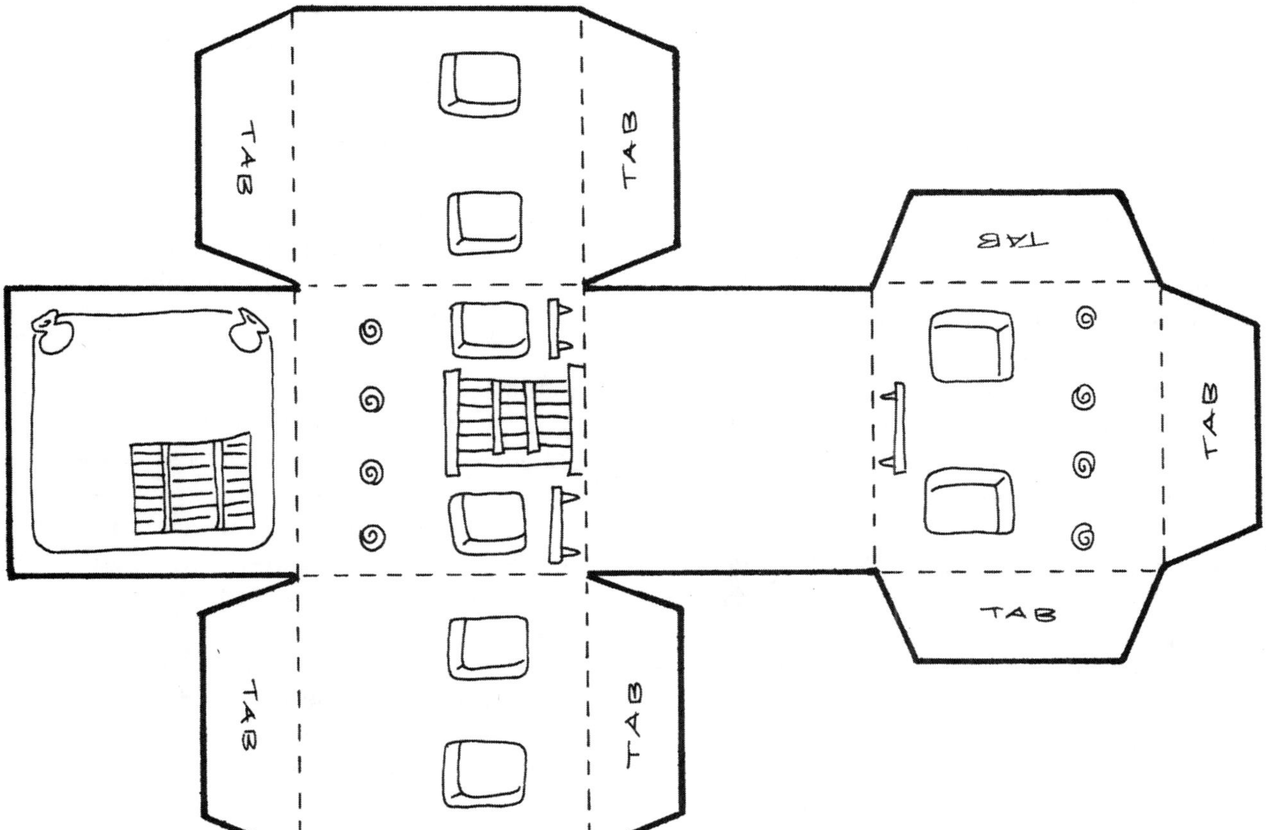

REPRODUCIBLE 9B

Lesson
10

All-in-One BIBLE FUN ELEMENTARY

The Sower

Bible Verse

I treasure your word in my heart.

Psalm 119:11

Bible Story

Matthew 13:3–8, 19–23

The parable of the sower is a good example of Jesus' use of the familiar to make a point with his listeners. Agriculture was a major business in Galilee, and sowing seed would have been a common sight.

Farmers owned grain fields adjacent to their neighbors, with boundaries marked only by a pile of stones. After preparing the soil by plowing it once if they thought it needed plowing, they would scatter fistfuls of seed over it with sweeping arm motions as they walked its length and breadth. Finally, they would plow a second time (in some cases, the first time) to cover the seed with dirt.

Inevitably as the seed was scattered, some of it would fall beyond the boundaries of the field, perhaps on a well-worn path at the field's edge or in soil that had not been prepared because it lay in a thin layer over rock. Jesus told his disciples that the various kinds of soil in his story represented the circumstances of those to whom the word of God was preached. Those who were represented by seed growing in good soil were those who heard God's word and acted on it.

The parable had a surprise ending for Jesus' listeners. The yields he suggested were far beyond the fifteenfold yield that would have been considered excellent in those times. Thus he was placing great value on hearing and obeying God's word.

Elementary children are beginning to recognize cause-and-effect relationships. They know that when you plant a seed and take care of it, a plant likely will grow. However, it may be difficult for them to make the connection that they are like good soil for the seeds of God's word.

Think of your teaching as a way to plant seeds of God's love. Help the children you teach know that by loving and obeying, by smiling and helping others, they are being the good soil that God wants them to be.

We can listen to God's Word and follow it.

If time is limited, we recommend those activities that are noted in **boldface**. Depending on your time and the number of children, you may be able to include more activities.

Activity	Time	Supplies	
Still Life Study	**15 minutes**	**paper towels, paper plates, construction paper (including green), green felt-tip markers, glue tempera paint, newspaper, smocks, spoons, hand-washing supplies**	Join the Fun
Mind Benders	5 minutes	Reproducible 8A, scissors	Join the Fun
Wonderful Dirt	5 minutes	dirt from various places, clear plastic containers with lids, water, paper plates, dried lima beans, resealable plastic bags, spoon, optional: magnifying glass	Bible Story Fun
Sing the Bible Verse	5 minutes	None	Bible Story Fun
Bible Story: The Sower	**5 minutes**	**newspaper, tape, boxes or blocks, blanket or sheet**	Bible Story Fun
Hair-Raising Seed	10 minutes	peat pots or small paper cups, potting soil, grass seed, spoons, feathers, ribbon, felt and fabric scraps, wiggle eyes, construction paper, water, glue, crayons or felt-tip markers	Bible Story Fun
Scatter the Seeds	10 minutes	Reproducible 10A, scissors, flower seeds, tape or glue, crayons or felt-tip markers	Bible Story Fun
Find the Treasure	5 minutes	Reproducible 10B, scissors, yarn	Live the Fun
Parable Prayers	**5 minutes**	**seed packet (Reproducible 10A)**	Live the Fun

Still Life Study

Supplies

paper towels, paper plates, construction paper (including green), green felt-tip markers, glue, tempera paint, newspaper, smocks, spoons, hand-washing supplies

Cut green construction paper into 2-inch by 11-inch strips. Cover the tables with newspaper. Set out several paper plates. Put a folded paper towel in each paper plate to make a paint pad. Provide green markers to color stems and leaves. Spoon tempera paint onto the paper towel pads.

As the children arrive, have the children put on paint smocks. Give each child a piece of construction paper and a strip of green construction paper. Show the children how to cut along the length of the strips as if they were making fringe. Have the children glue the fringe at the bottom of their paper plate to make grass.

Then let the children use the green felt-tip makers to draw stems and leaves growing up from the grass. When the leaves and stems have been drawn, let the children make thumbprints to add flowers to each stem. Show the children how to press a thumb onto the paint pad and then onto the top of a stem. This will make the middle of the flower. Encourage the children to make additional thumbprints around the middle thumbprint to complete the blossom. Have the children wash their hands.

When the children have completed their poster, let them write the Bible verse: I treasure your word in my heart (Psalm 119:11).

We can listen to God's Word and follow it.

Mind Benders

Supplies

Reproducible 8A, scissors

Photocopy and cut apart the objects (**Reproducible 8A**).

Say: Today's story has to do with remembering God's word. Let's see just how good your memory is.

Place the six pictures on a table or the floor. Let the children look at them and then ask them to turn around. Take the pictures away and let a child volunteer to put the pictures back on the table in the same order.

Another possibility is to place the six pictures on the table or rug, remove one while the children are turned around, and then let the children try to figure out which one is missing.

Wonderful Dirt

Supplies

dirt from various places, clear plastic containers with lids, water, paper plates, dried lima beans, resealable plastic bags, spoon, optional: magnifying glass

Prior to class, soak the dried lima beans overnight and then drain them. Collect different kinds of dirt—rich growing dirt, rocky soil, clay, sandy soil. Put each in a different plastic resealable bag for ease in transporting.

Put a few spoonfuls of dirt on each paper plate.

Ask: What do you think this is? *(dirt)* **Why do you think I brought dirt to the class today?** *(Who knows?)* **What would you say if I told you that Jesus compared us to different kinds of dirt? Did you know that there are different kinds of dirt?**

Let the children look at the different kinds of dirt. If you have magnifying glasses available, let the children look at the dirt with the glasses.

Ask: Which one is the darkest? Which one is the lightest? Which one has the most rocks in it? Which one has the most sand in it?

Put a scoopful of each of the different kinds of dirt into the clear containers. Pour enough water into each container to fill it more than half full. Put the lid on it. Have a child shake each container and then set the container back on the table. At the end of class look at the layers of material that has settled.

Say: We think dirt is just dirt. But there are different kinds of dirt. Suppose I were a seed. I wonder which kind of dirt I would prefer to grow in?

Give each child a lima bean. Let them pry the bean in half. Point out the tiny little plant inside.

Say: Every seed contains a little plant, ready to grow. Seeds grow best in soil that is fertile and able to receive the little seed. In our Bible story today Jesus tells us that we are like dirt.

Sing the Bible Verse

Supplies

None

Sing together the song printed below to the tune of "My Bonnie Lies Over the Ocean." Have the children stand up on the word "word" and sit back down on the word "heart." Sing the song several times, getting faster each time.

I treasure your word in my hear-t.
I treasure your word in my heart.
I treasure your word in my hear-t.
I treasure your word in my heart.

Trea-sure. Trea-sure.
I treasure your word in my heart,
my heart.
Trea-sure. Trea-sure.
I treasure your word in my heart.

The Sower

by LeeDell Stickler

You will need these characters: two birds, two seeds, sun, and three weeds

Set up these areas in the room: a path (three sheets of newspaper taped together, lengthwise), a rocky ground (boxes or blocks scattered around), a weed patch (newspaper crumpled and scattered about), and a field (a large blanket or sheet spread out).

Say: Jesus often told stories called *parables*. These stories were usually short and about something the people knew about. People in Bible times knew about growing food. Sowers often scattered seed all over the place, reaching into their sacks and casting the seed about.

One day a sower went out into the fields to plant. He scattered the seeds about.

Let's be sowers and scatter our seeds about. *(Let the children walk about the room and pretend to scatter seed. After a few minutes, bring the group back together. Walk about the room, beginning with the path.)*

Oh, look, there are some seeds that have fallen onto the path. They are just lying there on the top. They are just waiting for hungry birds to gobble them up for dinner. *(Birds gobble up the seeds.)*

Some seed has fallen here where the ground is rocky. But look, they are trying to grow. *(The two seeds stand on the rocky ground and begin to grow.)* They send up shoots and make green leaves.

But the summer sun is hot and beats down on them. The poor little seeds; their roots just aren't strong enough, and they wither up and die. *(Seeds die.)*

Some seed has fallen here into the weed patch. *(Seeds take their place in the weed patch.)* Look, they are growing. They send down roots and they send up shoots. How healthy they look. But what's that?

Weeds are growing up around them. *(The three weeds begin to grow.)* The weeds are choking them out. *(The weeds pretend to choke the seeds.)* Oh, poor little seeds, they are dying. *(Seeds die.)*

Oh, good, some seeds have fallen into the rich, dark soil of the field. *(Seeds grow.)* They send down tiny roots. They send up little shoots. They are protected from the hot summer sun. They have no weeds to choke them out. They take root and grow and grow and grow.

Jesus' parables always tried to teach the people a lesson. What do you think the seeds stood for? What are the disciples and Jesus sowing? *(the words of God)*

Sometimes when we tell people about God, our words fall on deaf ears. These people don't want to know about God and Jesus. They just go on their way and don't want salvation. What are those people in today's story? *(the path)*

There are some people who hear the words and listen at first, but at the first sign of trouble they run away. What are those people in today's story? *(the rocky ground)*

There are some people who hear the word and begin to be followers. But soon the cares of their lives pull them away and keep them from being followers. What are those people in today's story? *(the weed patch)*

But there are some people who hear the word, and the word grows in their hearts. It grows and grows and grows. And those people spread the word to others. What are those people in today's story? *(the fertile field)*

Which of those people do we want to be? *(those where God's word grows and grows and grows)*

Hair-Raising Seed

Supplies

peat pots or small paper cups, potting soil, grass seed, spoons, feathers, ribbon, felt and fabric scraps, wiggle eyes, construction paper, water, glue, crayons or felt-tip markers

Say: Jesus knew that the people were familiar with farming and sowing seeds. He wanted them to know that it wasn't enough just to hear the word of God. People had to live it every day of their life. Let's make a gift to take home to remind us that God's word will grow in our hearts.

Give each child a peat pot (or small paper cup). Have the children add bits of ribbon, felt scraps, wiggle eyes, construction paper, and fabric to make their pots into people.

When their faces are completed, let them add potting soil to within one-half inch of the top of the cups. Sprinkle about one to two teaspoons of grass seed on the dirt. Sprinkle with more potting soil. Tamp down and water slightly.

Say: We have given our seeds good dirt. Now if we water it lightly and provide it with warm sunshine, it will grow. As the grass seed begins to grow, it will look like hair. We are like this good soil: If we listen to God's word and follow it, then God's word will grow in our hearts.

We can listen to God's Word and follow it.

Scatter the Seeds

Supplies

Reproducible 10A, scissors, flower seeds, tape or glue, crayons or felt-tip markers

Photocopy the seed envelopes **(Reproducible 10A)** for each child.

Say: We can also spread God's word to others. Let's make seed packets so that other people can have God's word grow in their hearts as well.

Give each child a seed packet. Have the children cut out the envelope. Encourage them to decorate the envelopes with crayons or felt-tip markers.

Let the children place several flower seeds in each envelope. Help the children seal their envelopes with glue or tape.

Tell the children to give the packet of seeds to someone who needs to hear God's word.

Find the Treasure

Supplies

Reproducible 10B, scissors, yarn

Photocopy and cut apart the treasure slips **(Reproducible 10B)**. If you have more than eight children make extra copies of the slips.

Roll the slips into scrolls and tie each one with yarn. Hide the slips around the room.

Say: Our Bible verse today says that we are to treasure God's word in our heart. There are treasures hidden around the room. I want you to go on a treasure hunt. When you find one of the treasures, bring it with you to the worship area.

When everyone has found at least one "treasure," have them sit down in the worship area. Have the children open their tiny scrolls and read the treasured verse.

Say: Jesus told us to listen to God's word and follow it. If we follow God's word, what would we do in each of these verses.

Encourage the children to tell what they would do to follow their verse.

We can listen to God's Word and follow it.

Parable Prayers

Supplies

seed packet (Reproducible 10A)

Have the children sit down in a circle.

Show the children one of the seed packets **(Reproducible 10A)**.

Say: As the seed packet goes around the circle, I want each of you to say one thing that you will do this next week to show that you are hearing God's word and following it too.

Pray: Thank you, God, for stories Jesus told. Help us to learn from them just as people did long ago. Help us to listen to your word and to follow it. Amen.

I treasure your word in my heart.
Psalm 119:11
You shall love your neighbor as yourself.
Matthew 22:39
You shall love the Lord your God with all your heart.
Luke 10:27

Love your enemies, do good to those who hate you. (Luke 6:27)
Honor your father and mother. (Exodus 20:12)
A friend loves at all times. (Proverbs 17:17)
You shall love the Lord your God with all your heart. (Luke 10:27)
You shall love your neighbor as yourself. (Matthew 22:39)
Know that I am with you and will keep you wherever you go. (Genesis 28: 15)
This is my commandment, that you love one another as I have loved you. (John 15:12)
Forgive and you will be forgiven. (Luke 6:37)

REPRODUCIBLE 10B

Lesson

11

All-in-One BIBLE FUN ELEMENTARY

The Good Samaritan

Bible Verse

You shall love your neighbor as yourself.

Matthew 22:39

Bible Story

Luke 10:25–37

The story of the good Samaritan had a twist that surprised Jesus' audience. The hero was a Samaritan, a social outcast. While Samaritans worshiped the same God as the Jewish people, some of their religious traditions made them unacceptable to their more devout Jewish neighbors.

In the story the priest and the Levite had legitimate reasons for not helping their neighbor. In Jewish law anyone who touched a dead body was unclean for seven days. To become clean again required a ritual of purification. Perhaps the priest thought that if he touched the man, he would be unable to perform his priestly duties at the Temple. Obviously he thought his responsibilities were more important than aiding a man in distress. In addition the Levite also may have been worried about this being a setup for a robbery. The Jericho road was notorious for bandits, and Levites tended to be among the monied crowd.

The Samaritan, however, was not bound by the same strict religious laws as the priest and the Levite. He was free to help the injured man. In this story Jesus expressed concern that people were forgetting the need for compassion as they strived for righteousness.

Because of the media explosion in today's world, children are no longer bound by geographic borders. Everyone is our neighbor, whether that person lives next door or around the globe. This presents a new set of questions involving stewardship: How can we live so that our actions do not infringe upon the needs of others?

Explore with the children these questions: Who is my neighbor? How can we live so that we can be good neighbors to someone in another part of the world?

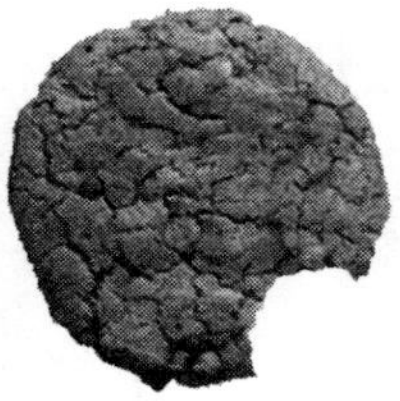

We can be good neighbors.

If time is limited, we recommend those activities that are noted in **boldface**. Depending on your time and the number of children, you may be able to include more activities.

Activity	Time	Supplies	
Action Theater	**10 minutes**	**Reproducibles 11A and 11B, felt-tip markers or crayons, scissors, tape or stapler, craft sticks or plastic straws, file folder or posterboard**	Join the Fun
Do the Jericho Jog	10 minutes	two shoe boxes, masking tape	Bible Story Fun
Over the Edge	5 minutes	five items found in your classroom such as paper cups, crayons, books, glue sticks, and paintbrushes	
Bible Story: The Good Neighbor	**10 minutes**	**None**	
Ring-a-ding-dong	10 minutes	paper plate, scissors, optional: index cards, felt-tip marker	
Sing the Bible Verse	5 minutes	None	
Who's My Neighbor?	5 minutes	yarn, scissors	Live the Fun
Parable Prayers	**5 minutes**	**Reproducible 11A, scissors**	

Supplies

Reproducibles 11A and 11B, felt-tip markers or crayons, scissors, tape or stapler, craft sticks or plastic straws, file folder or posterboard

Action Theater

Make a copy of the action puppets and background **(Reproducibles 11A and 11B)** for each child.

Greet the children as they arrive. Have the tables set up for the activity. Give each child a set of action theater puppets and the theater background. Have the children color and cut out each of the action characters: the priest, the Levite, the Samaritan, and his donkey.

When the children have finished coloring the characters, show the children how to fold them on the dotted line and staple or tape each side, forming a pocket. Slip a wooden craft stick or plastic drinking straw into the pocket for each character.

Prepare the background by cutting off the bottom part with the injured man as shown. Tape it on top of the background of the road, taping only the outside edges or the right and left sides as shown in the illustration.

To tell the story slip the action characters up through the open area, and move them "down the road."

To give this added stability, glue the background onto an old file folder or a piece of posterboard.

Say: In today's Bible story we learn about being neighbors. Two of the characters in the story have the chance to be good neighbors and don't. The other character has no reason to be a good neighbor, and yet he is.

We can be good neighbors.

Do the Jericho Jog

Supplies

two shoe boxes, masking tape

Set a beginning and ending line with masking tape. Remove the top of the shoeboxes. Set the two boxes on the floor.

Say: In today's Bible story there are many travelers going to Jericho. The Jericho road is a very dangerous road. Many thieves and robbers hid in the rocks around the curves of the road to attack unsuspecting travelers. Let's see if each of you can get to Jericho and back without being attacked by robbers.

Select one child to be the caller. The remainder of the children will be travelers. One half will stand in line at Jerusalem. The other half will stand in line at Jericho. The first child in the line at Jerusalem will step into the shoeboxes.

Say: The object is to get from Jerusalem to Jericho or from Jericho to Jerusalem. Each of you will have a turn as the traveler. The traveler steps into the shoeboxes and shuffles to the city. If the caller shouts out "robbers and thieves" then the traveler has only to the count of ten either to get back from the place he or she came or to the next city. If the traveler gets caught when the caller shouts, then the traveler gives the shoeboxes to the next traveler and goes to the end of the line at the city where he or she began.

Over the Edge

Supplies

five items found in your classroom such as paper cups, crayons, books, glue sticks, and paintbrushes

The object of this game is to work together to accomplish a certain task. Use masking tape to establish a beginning and ending line at opposite ends of the playing area. Set a table at the ending line. On the table place five items found in your classroom such as paper cups, crayons, books, glue sticks, and paintbrushes.

Divide the children into pairs. Let them decide who will be the balancer and who will be the supporter on the first round.

Say: When I say "go," the teams will go to the table, balance one item on the balancer's head, and come back to the starting line. The balancer and supporter will change places. Then the teams will go to the table, balance two items on the balancer's head or shoulders, and come back. This continues until the teams complete five items. The first team to get five items wins. If an item falls off the balancer's head or shoulders, then it is up to the support person to put it back on.

This game will show the children how important it is to help one another.

The Good Neighbor

by James Ritchie

The story of the good Samaritan is very familiar to many children. A man is beset by robbers and lies by the side of the road waiting for someone to help him. Finally someone stops to help. The one who stops to help is a stranger who probably wouldn't have been expected to help.

To make it even more fun, perform the story as a rap. Assign one of the verses to each child. The entire class will do the refrain. Please note the rhythm of the refrain as indicated by the musical notes. Establish a rhythm with the stanzas.

Good Samaritan Rap

Refrain

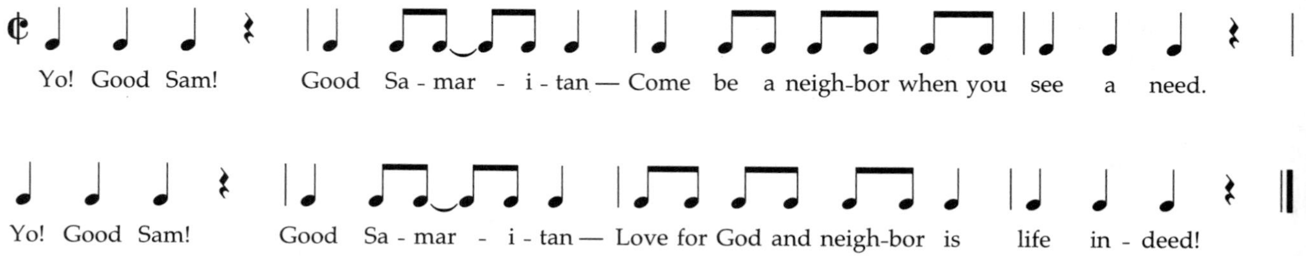
Yo! Good Sam! Good Sa - mar - i - tan — Come be a neigh-bor when you see a need.
Yo! Good Sam! Good Sa - mar - i - tan — Love for God and neigh-bor is life in - deed!

1. A traveler left Jerusalem,
to start this episode.
He set his sights on Jericho
and headed down the road.

2. But crouching in the shadows
hid behind a wall of stone,
a band of robbers waited
for someone to pass alone.

3. "Let's get him!" yelled the
leader, as the man looked up in
dread.
The robbers stripped and beat
him,
and they left him almost dead.

Refrain

4. By chance a priest was going
down
the road to Jericho.
He took a look and passed on by
as quick as he could go.

5. A Levite also came that way
but never broke his stride.
He saw the beaten traveler
and hugged the other side.

6. And then came a Samaritan,
an outcast through and through.
Surprise! He was the one who
stopped
to see what he could do.

Refrain

7. With oil and wine he cleaned
the wounds,
so moved was he within;
then put the man upon his
beast,
and took him to the inn.

8. All night he nursed the injured
man,
then with the morning sun,
he asked the keeper of the inn
to do as he had done.

9. "If you will take good care of
him,
I'll come this way again
and pay you for your services,"
said the Samaritan.

Refrain

Words and Music: James Ritchie ©1993 Cokesbury

Ask: Why was the man injured? *(He had been attacked by robbers.)* **Who stopped to help him?** *(the Samaritan)* **What did the Samaritan do?** *(He took care of the man's injuries. In the morning he took him to an inn and asked the innkeeper to take care of him.)*

Say: When Jesus told this story, it was shocking to the people. Samaritans were looked down on. A Samaritan doing something good and being held up as an example? This was impossible! But that is what Jesus wanted the people to know. God wanted them to be good neighbors, not just to people they knew, but to all people.

Ring-a-ding-dong

Supplies

paper plate, scissors, optional: index cards, felt-tip marker

Cut the center out of a paper plate to make a ring.

Select five children to be the seven words for today's Bible verse: "You shall love your neighbor as yourself" (Matthew 22:39). Whisper one word in each one's ear. Then have them sit in the center of the room with their hands together over their head, forming a ringtoss post. Have the remainder of the children line up.

The first child will toss the paper plate ring over the hands of one of the seated children. The child will shout out the word the teacher whispered in his or her ear. If it is the first word in the Bible verse, then the child will toss the ring a second time. The player continues as long as the words are in order. When a wrong word is called out, then turn passes to one of another child.

When one child completes the Bible verse, he or she trades places with one of the ringtoss children. The teacher mixes up the words again and play can begin again. If the game goes slowly, play through only one time. If you would like to keep track of the words, make several sets on index cards. Let each child hold their word and give it to the one who rings him or her if the word is in the correct order.

We can be good neighbors.

Sing the Bible Verse

Supplies

None

Encourage the children to sing the Bible verse to the tune of "She'll Be Coming 'Round the Mountain." Speak the words printed in italics at the end of each phrase. Repeat the song and let the children stomp their feet and bump their hips together instead of speaking the words.

O-o you shall love your neighbor as yourself. *(Yes, Lord!)*
O-o you shall love your neighbor as yourself. *(That's right!)*
O-o you shall love your neighbor,
O-o you shall love your neighbor,
O-o you shall love your neighbor as yourself. *(Yes, Lord! That's right!)*

O-o you shall love your neighbor as yourself. *(stomp, stomp)*
O-o you shall love your neighbor as yourself. *(bump bump)*
O-o you shall love your neighbor,
O-o you shall love your neighbor,
O-o you shall love your neighbor as yourself. *(stomp, stomp, bump, bump)*

Who's My Neighbor?

Supplies

yarn, scissors

Bring the children together in a circle. Roll yarn into a ball.

Say: In our Bible story we talked about neighbors. Even though the Priest and the Levite were technically neighbors to the man who was injured, they did not stop to help. The Samaritan, who technically was a foreigner, did stop and help. The Samaritan was the good neighbor.

Say: I am going to hold this ball of yarn. You are going to ask me: "Who is your neighbor?" I will name someone and toss the ball to them, continuing to hold onto a part of the yarn. The group will ask the person I threw it to: "Who is your neighbor?" That person will name someone and toss the ball to him or her, continuing to hold onto a part of the yarn. We will continue until everyone is holding onto a part of the yarn.

When everyone is connected, **say: We are all neighbors, even though we do not live next door to each other or even on the same street. We are neighbors with persons who live in our city, our state, our country. We are neighbors with persons who live in this country or in countries far away. God wants us to care about our neighbors, no matter where they are.**

As you reroll the yarn, cut small portions of the yarn (about six inches long) and tie it around each child's wrist as a reminder to be a good neighbor.

Parable Prayers

Supplies

Reproducible 11A, scissors

Have the children stand together in a group. Photocopy and cut out the Samaritan puppet **(Reproducible 11A)**.

Ask: What did the story Jesus told teach us? *(We can be good neighbors.)*

Say: There are many ways we can be good neighbors. As we pass the Samaritan puppet around the circle, think of some way you can be a good neighbor. I will start. I will try to be patient when I drive from place to place. *(Pass the Samaritan puppet to the next person.)*

If a child cannot think of any way to be a good neighbor, let him or her pass. When everyone has had a chance to pass the Samaritan puppet, have the children join hands and raise them above their heads. Say the Bible verse aloud.

Pray: Dear God, we know that we are all your children, no matter where we live. Help us to love one another, and help us to be good neighbors. Amen.

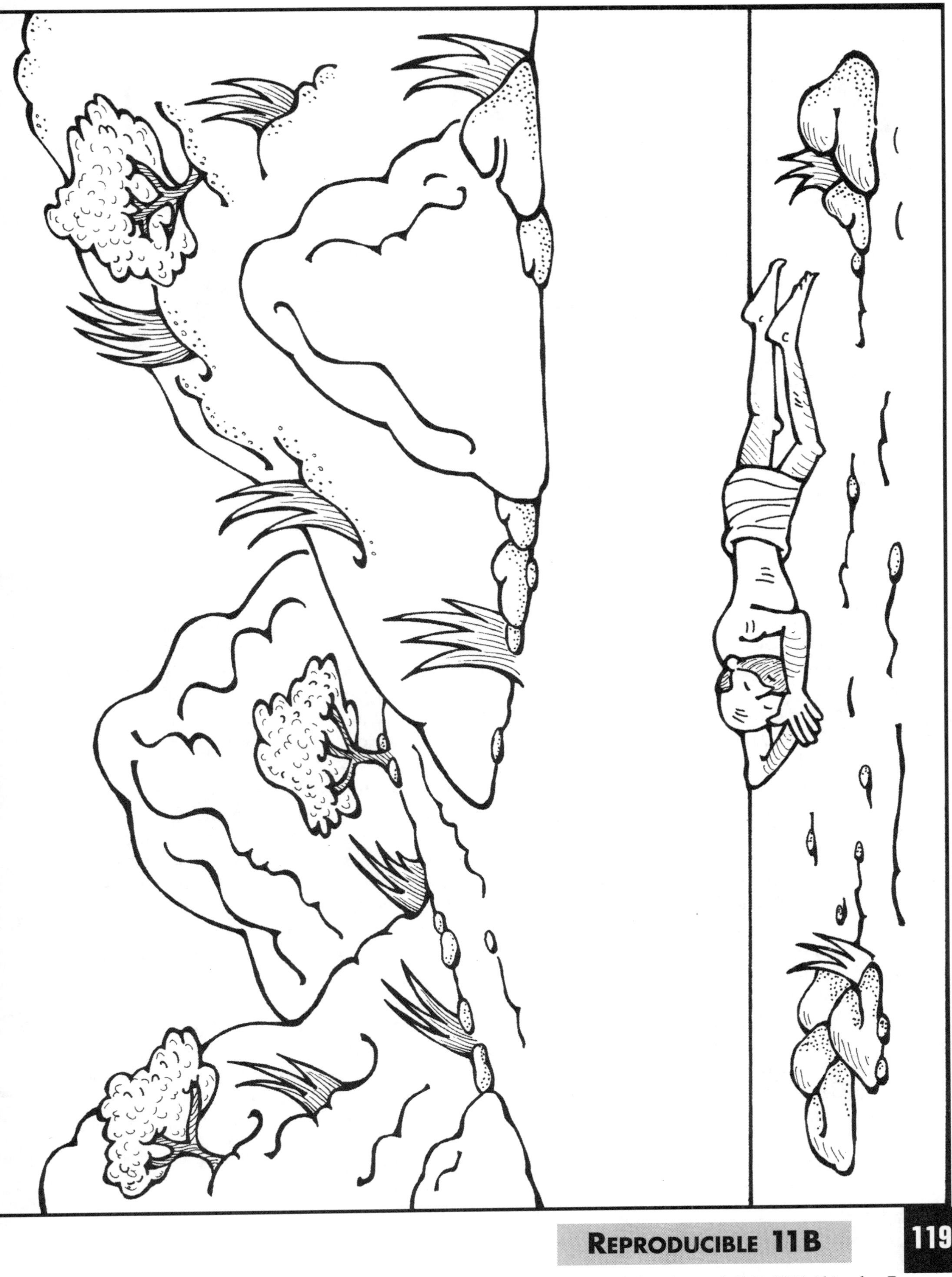

The Lost Sheep

Bible Verse

The LORD is my shepherd, I shall not want.

Psalm 23:1

Bible Story

Matthew 18:12–14

A shepherd's job was to care for sheep. Shepherds protected the flock from dangerous animals. Shepherds led the flock to calm, shallow water. Shepherds found pastures of fresh, green grass for the sheep to eat. A shepherd would risk his life to care for the sheep in his flock. Every sheep was important, every single one. Psalm 23 compares God to a good shepherd.

In his stories Jesus often used common, everyday images to help the people understand what he was trying to say. Shepherds and sheep were common in Palestine. A flock of one hundred sheep would have been a fairly good-sized flock for a single shepherd. How the people must have gasped when Jesus told about a shepherd who would leave ninety-nine sheep and go after one lost one. What would happen to the other sheep while the shepherd was away?

But Jesus wanted the people to understand that each of them was important to God, important enough to risk the other ninety-nine in order to find the one who was lost. God seeks people out, like the shepherd who searched for his sheep. God rejoices in the rescue of just one person, like the shepherd who rejoiced when his sheep was found.

Children have basic needs. They need food to eat, a place to live, shelter, and clothing to keep them warm. But these are not the only needs of a child. They have emotional and spiritual needs as well. Every child needs to feel important. Children need to believe that someone cares about what they do and where they are. This concrete example of love helps them better understand God's love.

Continually remind the children you teach that they are loved and that they are important—not only to you, but also to God. Rejoice in the children just as God rejoices in them. Pray for those "lost" children in your class who are not as easy to love. Ask for God's help in showing them love, because they probably need it most of all.

God loves us and cares about us.

If time is limited, we recommend those activities that are noted in **boldface**. Depending on your time and the number of children, you may be able to include more activities.

Activity	Time	Supplies	
Sheep Shape	**10 minutes**	**Reproducibles 12A and 12B. posterboard (eight inches by eighteen inches), crayons, scissors, quart-sized reseal-able plastic bags, glue, small paper cups, craft sticks, kitchen timer, magnetic strips, optional: paper clips**	JOIN THE FUN
Baa, Baa, Baa	5 minutes	blindfold, chair	
Sheep in the Dark	10 minutes	Reproducible 12B, scissors, tape, 2 blindfolds	BIBLE STORY FUN
Sheep Roundup	10 minutes	red, yellow, green construc-tion paper squares, masking tape	
Bible Story: The Shepherd and the Lost Sheep	**10 minutes**	**None**	
Make a Thaumatrope	10 minutes	Reproducible 12A, plastic drinking straws or pencils, scissors, tape, crayons or felt-tip markers, glue	
What's Missing?	10 minutes	ten items from your class-room such as crayons, mark-ers, scissors, books, glue, paper, pencils, pens, paint-brushes, and paper cups	
Sing the Bible Verse	5 minutes	Bibles	LIVE THE FUN
Parable Prayers	**5 minutes**	**None**	

Sheep Shape

Supplies

Reproducibles 12A and 12B. posterboard (eight inches by eighteen inches), crayons, scissors, quart-sized resealable plastic bags, glue, small paper cups, craft sticks, kitchen timer, magnetic strips, optional: paper clips

Make a copy of the sheep shape game **(Reproducibles 12A and 12B)** for each team of two to three children.

Greet the children as they arrive. Divide the children into teams of three or two. Let each team prepare one game set.

Give each team a piece of posterboard. Have each team glue the sheepfold at one end of the posterboard sheet. Let the teams cut out and assemble the sheep. (If you have a large class, rather than using the magnetic strips on the individual sheep as shown in the directions, use paper clips. Glue a piece of the magnetic strip to the end of a craft stick.)

Place each game board on four cups, one at each corner. This leaves the underside almost totally open. The children will take turns trying to see how many sheep can be coaxed into the pen within a certain time limit. Move the craft stick beneath the posterboard to capture sheep. Drag the sheep using the magnetic strip into the sheepfold. Use a kitchen timer and give each child one minute. Make sure every child has an opportunity to be the shepherd. After playing the game, store each set of the game in a resealable plastic bag.

Say: It is very important for a shepherd to get all his sheep into the sheepfold before nightfall. There are many dangerous animals that would love to have lamb chops for dinner. A shepherd takes good care of his or her sheep. Today's Bible story compares God's love to that of the love of a shepherd.

God loves us and cares about us.

Baa, Baa, Baa

Supplies

blindfold, chair

Bring the children together in a large circle. Select one child to be the shepherd. The shepherd will sit in the center chair with a blindfold on. The teacher will call on different children to come to the shepherd and say, "Baa, baa." The shepherd will try to discover who each sheep is. If the shepherd guesses the identity of the sheep, the sheep becomes the next shepherd.

Say: In Bible times the sheep would know the voice of their shepherd. Many sheep might be grazed together, sheep that belonged to different owners. But when the shepherd called his sheep, they would recognize the shepherd's voice and follow eagerly.

Sheep in the Dark

Supplies

Reproducible 12B, scissors, tape, 2 blindfolds

Photocopy and cut out two of the sheep game pieces (**Reproducible 12B**). Assemble the sheep as shown.

Divide the children into two teams. Have each team form a circle sitting on the floor. Select a representative of each team to be the shepherd. Have each shepherd move to the center of his or her circle. Blindfold the shepherds.

Once the shepherds are wearing the blindfolds, give each team a sheep figure. Have the teams hide their sheep in their circles.

Say: Our two shepherds have lost a sheep and must crawl on their hands and knees to find it. The sheep figures will be our lost sheep. Each team will be the helpers, trying to help the shepherd. One team will make a cheeping sound like a little bird. The closer their shepherd gets to the lamb, the louder the cheeping. The other team will make a sound like a frog makes. The closer their shepherd gets to the lamb, the louder the ribbiting. *(Enclose the circle with children so the two blindfolded shepherds cannot get out of the circle.)* **All right, shepherds, go find your lost sheep.**

Play until one of the shepherds has found the sheep. Then choose two new shepherds and play again. Play until each child has had a chance to be a shepherd.

Sheep Roundup

Supplies

red, yellow, green (or more colors) construction paper squares, masking tape

Tape a colored construction paper square onto each child. There should be at least four of each color, so if you have fewer than twelve children, then only use two colors. For larger classes, use more than three colors. Select one of each color to be the shepherd. The remainder of the children will be sheep and should make appropriate noises. Make a cone of the different colors of construction paper. Set the cone on the opposite side of the room on the floor.

Say: Often the sheep of several shepherds would be sheltered together in the evening. But when the time came to go into the hills, each shepherd called out his own flock. When I say "scatter," all the sheep will scatter in the room and will freeze in place when I say "halt." The shepherd will then rush around and try to find all the sheep that have the same color as the shepherd. Whenever a shepherd tags a sheep, the sheep holds onto the waist of the shepherd as the shepherd continues to find his or her sheep. When a shepherd has all the sheep, the shepherd and sheep run to the colored cone.

Play until a shepherd has picked up a cone. Then reassemble and play again. Select different shepherds.

The Shepherd and the Lost Sheep

by LeeDell Stickler

Jesus told the story of the Lost Sheep so that people could understand what God's love was like. He used familiar items so that making the connection would be easy. The people knew about sheep and shepherds. They knew just what a shepherd did to care for his sheep. But there is a special twist to the story. See if you can figure it out.

Say: I want you to pretend to be the sheep. Get down on your hands and knees. And between the stanzas of the poem, I want you to say: "Baa, baa."

Practice with the children so they know how to make the sound.

Once there was a shepherd
who had one hundred sheep.
He found cool water for them to
drink
and green grass for them to eat.

Response: Baa, baa.

He cared for all his sheep
And kept them safe from harm.
He built a pen of sticks and stones
To keep them dry and warm.

"Come, little sheep," the shepherd
called,
"Let's go out for the day.
The sun is warm and the grass is
fresh.
You can run and play," he said.

Response: Baa, baa.

"And when the sun begins to set
And the sky's no longer light,
We'll come back down the
mountainside,
together for the night."

Response: Baa, baa.

One, two, three, four, five, and six
Seven, eight, and nine.
The shepherd counted every one
'Till he got to ninety-nine.

Response: Baa, baa.

"I must have counted wrong,"
he said,
And counted them again.
But all he found were ninety-nine
Standing in the pen.

Response: Baa, baa.

"There were one hundred sheep
this morning!"
He cried in great distress.
"If one is missing from the flock,
I'll be in such a mess."

Response: Baa, baa.

The shepherd left the ninety-nine
To search for the one lost sheep.
He had to find the missing one,
Before he went to sleep.

Response: Baa, baa.

"He could have fallen off the cliff
Or been eaten by a bear.
He could have fallen in the stream
And drowned with me not there."

Response: Baa, baa.

"There you are!" the shepherd
said,
When the little lost one he spied.
"Don't move a muscle or you will
fall,"
The frightened shepherd cried.

Response: Baa, baa.

He scooped the missing sheep
right up
Into his waiting arms.
"I'll take you home," the shepherd
said.
"Back where it's safe and warm."

Response: Baa, baa.

"Let's celebrate," the shepherd
said.
"I've found my little lost sheep.
And now that all are home again,
I know that I can sleep."

When Jesus told this story
To people long ago,
He wanted them to know
That God does love them so.

Response: Baa, baa.

Supplies

Reproducible 12A, plastic drinking straws or pencils, scissors, tape, crayons or felt-tip markers, glue

Make a Thaumatrope

Make a copy of the sheep and shepherd thaumatrope **(Reproducible 12A)** for each child.

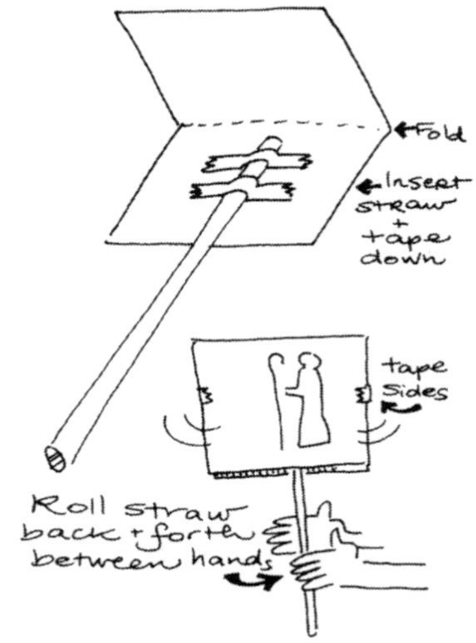

The word *thaumatrope* comes from two Greek words that mean "wonder" and "to turn." The thaumatrope has two pictures back to back. When the pictures are spun, they look like they become one picture.

Have the children cut out the activity and fold on the dotted line. Color the shepherd and the sheep. (Do not add any background. Just keep the figures.)

Place a straw (or pencil) on the inside of the folded square. Tape the straw or pencil securely. Put a little white glue on the three edges and press together, enclosing the straw or pencil inside. Allow to dry slightly.

Have the children hold the straw or pencil between the palms of their hands. Gently roll back and forth. As the picture spins, the shepherd and the sheep will appear to come together as one picture.

Say: God's love for us is like the love of a shepherd for his sheep. We are very important to God, never out of God's sight, even for a moment.

Supplies

ten items from your classroom such as crayons, markers, scissors, books, glue, paper, pencils, pens, paintbrushes, and paper cups

What's Missing?

Gather the children around the table. Set out ten items on the table. Have the children look at the items on the table.

Have the children turn away from the table. Remove one item. Have the children turn back. Select a child who thinks he or she knows what is missing. Do this several times, then begin to remove two items or three items.

Ask: Was it easy or hard to determine what was missing?

Say: The lost sheep is a story that Jesus told to teach the people a lesson.

Ask: How did the shepherd feel about the missing sheep? *(The sheep was very important.)* **What did he do?** *(He left everything and went in search of the sheep.)* **How did the shepherd feel when he found the lost sheep.** *(He was very happy.)* **What did Jesus tell us about God in this story?** *(God loves and cares about each of us just as the shepherd cared about his sheep.)*

Sing the Bible Verse

Supplies

Bibles

Say: Our Bible verse today is from the Psalms.

Have the children turn to Psalm 23 in their Bibles. Remind the children that the Book of Psalms is in the middle of the Bible.

Say: The shepherd boy David wrote Psalm 23, which is sometimes called "The Shepherd's Psalm." David understood that God's love for us is like the love of a shepherd for his sheep.

God loves us and cares about us.

Sing the song printed below to the tune of "The Wheels on the Bus."

The Lord is my shepherd, I'll not want.
I'll not want. I'll not want.
The Lord is my shepherd, I'll not want.
I shall not want.

Parable Prayers

Supplies

None

Bring the children together in the worship circle.

Ask: How do we know that God loves us and cares about us? *(God gives us family, friends, home, shelter, people to love and care about us.)*

Say: Today's Bible verse says that the Lord will provide for us all that we need. We just have to trust God. For our closing prayer I am going to say a sentence, and then I want you to respond with the second part of the verse: "I shall not want." When we get to the end of the prayer, we will say it all together.

Pray: The Lord is my shepherd
Response: I shall not want.
The Lord gives me a place to live.
Response: I shall not want.
The Lord gives me food to eat.
Response: I shall not want.
The Lord gives me a family.
Response: I shall not want.
The Lord gives me friends.
Response: I shall not want.
All: The Lord is my shepherd, I shall not want. Amen.

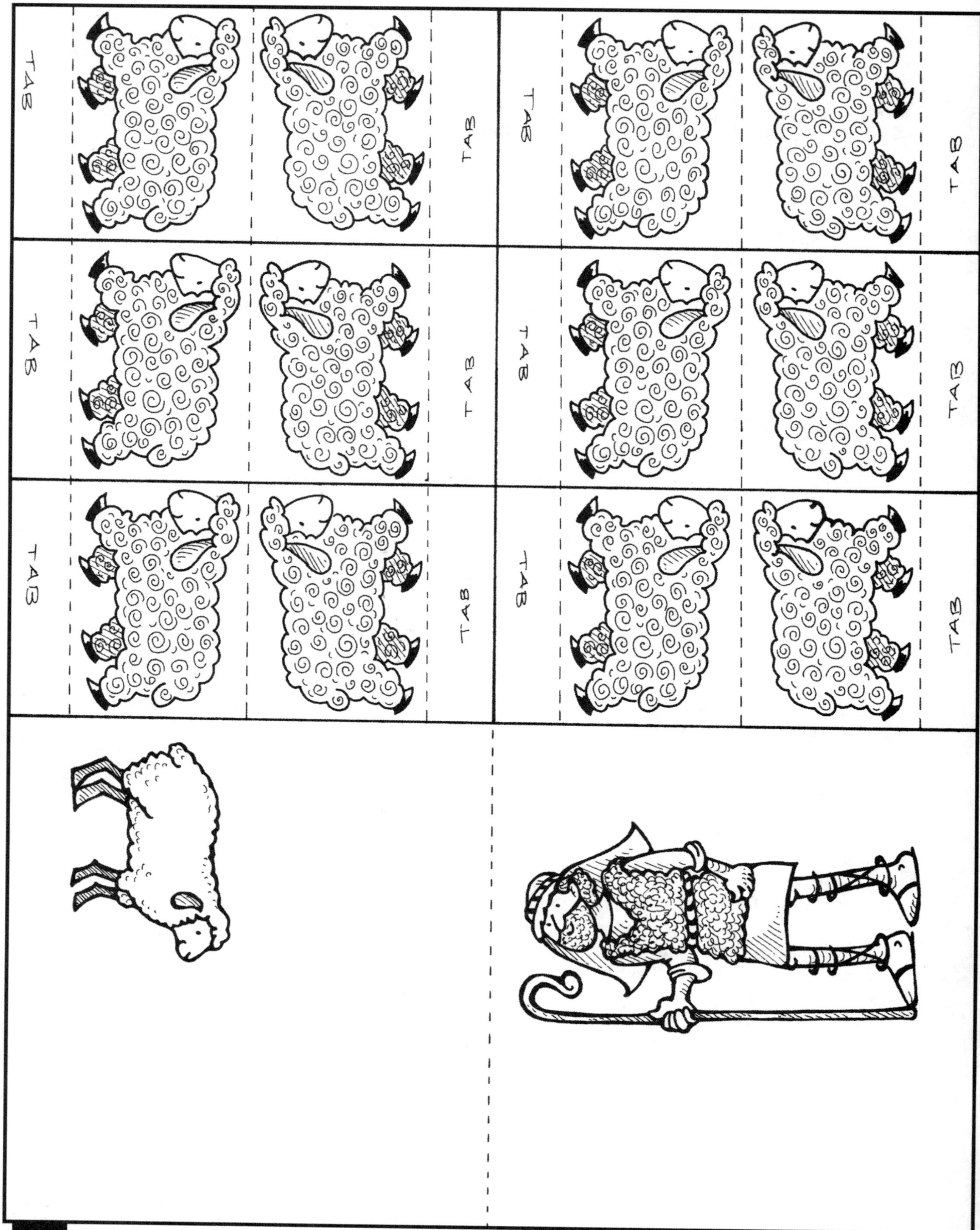
TAB
TAB
TAB
TAB
TAB
TAB
TAB
TAB
TAB
TAB
TAB
TAB

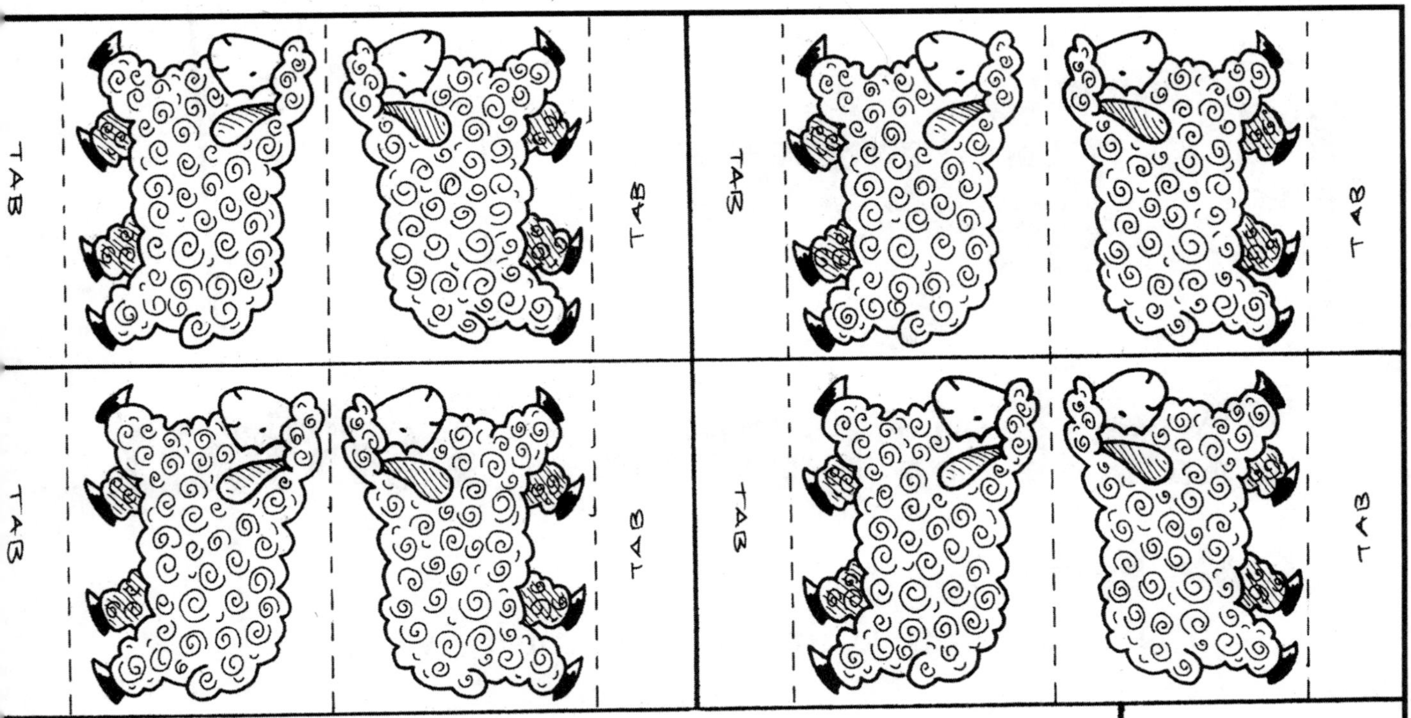

Fold + tape on underside

Glue magnet to-the inside

REPRODUCIBLE 12B

The Forgiving Father

Bible Verse

For you, O LORD, are good and forgiving.

Psalm 86:5

Bible Story

Luke 15:11–32

In today's story Jesus compares God to a parent. The two brothers represent two kinds of people—those who are always faithful, and those who stray but return to being faithful.

Arrogantly, the younger son took his inheritance and squandered it. Finding himself desperate, he took a job as a swineherd. Pork was a forbidden meat for the Jewish people, so for a Jewish boy to have taken such a job meant he had truly reached the lowest of the low. Near starvation, the younger son returned to his family, hoping only to be treated as a servant. The father, laying aside all dignity, ran to embrace his lost son and welcome him home, not as a servant, but as a son.

But the older brother was less than excited about his brother's return. And many people identify with his feelings. He did not squander his inheritance. He was the obedient son. His father assured him, however, that he had been appreciated, and that, while the love was not tested, the love was still there nonetheless.

While children are younger, parents and adults often make most of their decisions for them. But as they grow, more and more decision-making is thrust upon them. Many children will have experienced times when they have made wrong choices and had to pay the consequences for them. The one constant they need to be aware of is that when they make a poor choice, it is the choice that is bad not them.

Reassure the children that they are loved. God does not keep score. No matter how many times a child may make mistakes, God continues to love, accept, and forgive him or her.

God forgives us when we do wrong.

If time is limited, we recommend those activities that are noted in **boldface**. Depending on your time and the number of children, you may be able to include more activities.

Activity	Time	Supplies	
Bible Story Puppets	**10 minutes**	**Reproducibles 13A and 13B, scissors, crayons or felt-tip markers, glue, tape, dark yarn, optional: square of fabric or scarf for each puppet**	Join the Fun
Stick!	5 minutes	None	
Pay the Price	10 minutes	Reproducible 13A (left side), scissors, basket or bag, trash can, newspaper	Bible Story Fun
Sing the Bible Story	5 minutes	None	
Bible Story: The Forgiving Father	**5 minutes**	**Bible story puppets (Reproducibles 13A and 13B), table or sheet and two chairs, paper for deed, plastic coins, sandals, pouch**	
Welcome Home!	10 minutes	None	
Ring-a-ding Verse	5 minutes	paper plate, scissors, piece of paper for each child, index cards, felt-tip markers, masking tape	
Sign a Prayer	5 minutes	None	Live the Fun
Parable Prayers	**5 minutes**	**None**	

Supplies

Reproducibles 13A and 13B, scissors, crayons or felt-tip markers, glue, tape, dark yarn, optional: square of fabric or scarf for each puppet

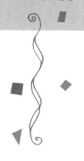

Bible Story Puppets

Photocopy the puppet faces **(Reproducibles 13A and 13B)** for each child. Or if you have a small class, make one set and let the children work together on each puppet.

Greet the children. Let the children color and then cut out the puppet faces and paper strips. Let the children create beards and hair for the characters. Snip small pieces of dark yarn. Then rub them together until the bits become fuzzy. Put glue on the areas of the puppets where hair and beards are indicated. Press the fuzzy yarn onto these places.

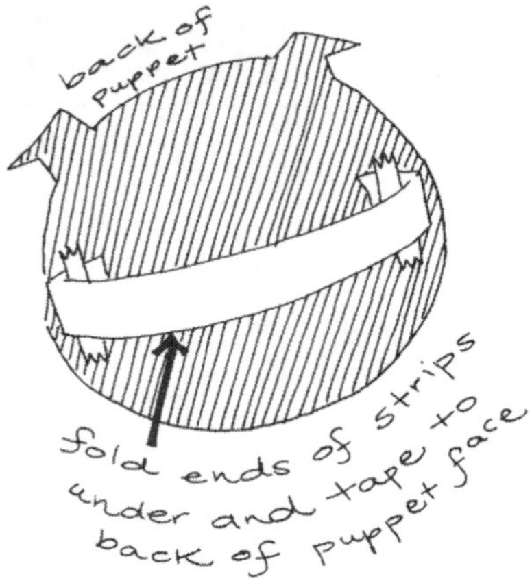

Have the children use the strips to make holders on the backs of the puppets. Have the children fold under both ends of each paper strip. Tape the folded part of the strips on to the backs of the puppet faces. Let the holder dry.

Show the children how to slip a scarf over their hands and then slip their hands up into the puppet faces, creating garments for the puppets.

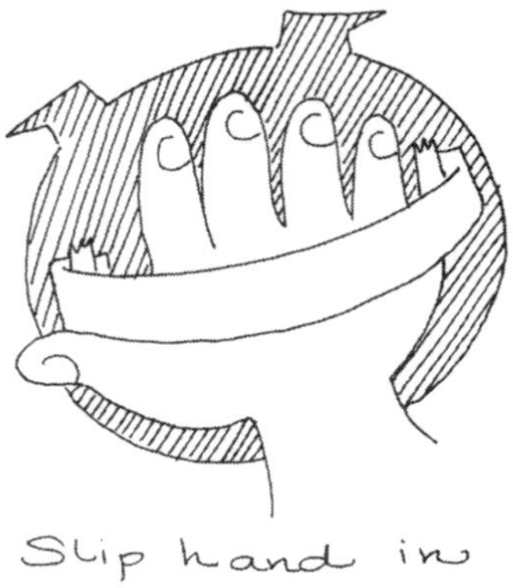

Set aside the puppets until time for the Bible story.

Supplies

None

Stick!

The object of this game is to group the whole class in a clump. Have the children stand in a circle.

Say: As we read the Bible, one of the things we learn about God is that God really sticks with us. God is always there for us. No matter what we've done wrong, God will forgive us. Let's play a game called "Stick." This game will remind us of just how close God is to us. I will call out a characteristic. All those people who have that characteristic will "stick" together. The people can hold hands or they can attach themselves by touching in some other way.

Call out these characteristics: children wearing tennis shoes, children wearing red, children who are wearing stripes, children who like ice cream. End the game with this characteristic: children who are loved by God.

Pay the Price

Photocopy and cut apart the consequences page **(Reproducible 13A)**. Place them in a basket or bag.

Place a trash can in the center of the room. Have the children form a circle around it no more than ten feet from the can.

Give each child several sheets of newspaper. Have the children crumple the newspaper into balls.

Say: Even though God will always forgive us when we do wrong, God does not keep us from paying the price whenever we do wrong.

Ask: What would happen if you decided to jump off a cliff? *(get squashed)* **What would happen if you ate nothing but sweets?** *(your teeth would rot)* **What would happen if you jumped into a pit of rattlesnakes?** *(get bitten)*

Say: God has given each of us a brain to make choices. When we make poor choices, God will forgive us. But God doesn't keep us from having to deal with the consequences of those choices. Let's play a game. In this game you are trying to toss the newspaper ball into the trash can. There's only one catch. If you miss, then you must pay the price.

Let the children take turns trying to toss their paper balls in the can. If a child misses, then he or she draws a consequence and does it.

Say: In today's Bible story, one of our characters makes a poor choice and has to pay the consequences. But at the end, everything is just great.

Supplies

Reproducible 13A (left side), scissors, basket or bag, trash can, newspaper

God forgives us when we do wrong.

Sing the Bible Story

Sing the song printed below to the tune of "She'll Be Coming 'Round the Mountain."

O-o, Jesus told a story about God.
O-o, Jesus told a story about God.
He said God was like a father,
He said God was like a father,
He said God was like a father,
who forgives.

Supplies

None

The Forgiving Father

by LeeDell Stickler

Assign parts and act out the story of the forgiving father as a puppet play. Create a stage by turning a table over on its side. Or you can drape a sheet between two chairs. Make a copy of the script for each player.

Narrator: Jesus told this story to help people understand what God was like. He wanted people to know that God forgave them when they did something wrong.

There was a father who had two sons. The older son was hardworking and obedient. *(Older son acts as though working hard.)* The younger son was impatient and reckless. *(Younger son taps hands impatiently.)*

Younger Son: Father, I know that someday part of your land will be mine. I'm young. I've got a lot of living to do. I don't want to wait.

Narrator: Now the father loved both of his sons very much. He knew that his youngest son was making a poor choice, but he wanted to make his son happy.

Father: Here is the deed to your part of the land. *(Hands son the deed.)* You can sell it and take the money, if that's your wish.

Younger Son: I'm tired of being a farmer. I think I'll sell the land.

Narrator: And that's just what he did. Now the youngest son headed for the big city with a pocket full of gold.

Younger Son: *(Walks and whistles.)*

City Slicker: *(aside)* Here comes a tourist if I ever saw one! *(to the younger son)* Hello there, young fellow. You look like a man who would be interested in a deal.

Younger Son: What kind of deal?

City Slicker: Dangerous threads. You can't go to the big city looking like a country boy.

Younger Son: *(Trades coins for new clothes and starts walks down the road whistling to himself.)*

City Slicker: Where are your wheels? No one in the city walks these days. What you need are some killer wheels.

Younger Son: *(Trades coins for donkey.)*

City Slicker: Tsk, tsk, tsk.

Younger Son: What's wrong now?

City Slicker: Those shoes are a disgrace.

Younger Son: *(Trades coins for new sandals.)*

City Slicker: How about a place to stay? I know this great little inn just down the road.

Younger Son: *(Holds up empty purse.)*

Narrator: When the younger son ran out of money, he also ran out of friends. *(City Slicker walks away leaving younger son alone.)*

Younger Son: I have no money. I have no food to eat. What can I do?

Narrator: Finally the younger son went to a farmer who raised pigs.

Younger Son: *(to pig farmer)* I need a job so that I can eat. Do you have work for me?

Farmer: You can feed my pigs. And if there's anything left over, you can eat it yourself.

Narrator: The younger son was so unhappy. He had no money, no friends, no home, no food. He had to take the job.

Younger Son: *(sitting in the muck with the pigs.)* Even my father's servants live better than this. I'm going back home. If I cannot be his son again, then I'll be a servant.

Narrator: So the younger son said goodbye to the pigs and started out for home. When the boy came near his father's house, he received a big surprise. His father came running out to greet him.

Father: Welcome home, son. I'm so glad you've returned.

Younger Son: Father, I'm so sorry.

Father: I'm just glad you're home. We're going to have a party to celebrate.

Narrator: And the people who heard this story learned that like the forgiving father in the story, God forgave them whenever they did wrong.

Welcome Home!

Supplies

None

Bring the children together in an open area.

Say: The younger son made a few mistakes in his life. He paid the price. But he was sorry and wanted to come home.

Ask: What did his father do when he came home? *(He welcomed him.)* **How did the younger son feel?** *(good)*

Say: Let's play a game called "Welcome Home!" I will select one person to be the father. The father will sit in a chair facing the group. We'll be the younger son. We'll ask our father: "Can we come home?" Father will put his hand up to his ear and ask: "What did you say?" We will take a step closer and repeat the question. Every time the father asks us to repeat the question, we have to take a step closer. When father finally says "Yes," then he jumps up and tries to catch us. We try to escape.

Play the game several times, allowing other children to play the part of the forgiving father.

Ring-a-ding Verse

Supplies

paper plate, scissors, piece of paper for each child, index cards, felt-tip markers, masking tape

Cut the center out of a paper plate. Write each child's name on a piece of paper. Tape the pieces of paper around the wall. This will be the Bible verse collection.

Write each word of the Bible verse on a separate index card. Put a loop of masking tape on the back of each card. Place the cards on the floor around the open area of the room. Make sure there is at least two to three feet of space between each card.

Have the children form a circle around the cards.

Say: We're going to see if we can ring the Bible verse. We'll begin with the first word of the Bible verse. Who can remember what it is? *(For).*

You will toss the paper plate ring over the word "For." If the word shows in the circle of the ring, then you can go and write that word on your Bible verse collection poster. If you miss, you'll have to wait until the next time. The turn will pass to the next person.

Let the children stand close enough that there will be only few misses. However, the word must be totally visible in the circle of the ring. The teacher will make the judgment calls. The first person to ring all eight of the words in order is the winner.

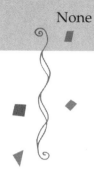

Sign a Prayer

Supplies

None

Have the children sit in a circle. Teach the children the sign language for "I'm sorry."

I'm—Hold the pinky finger up while holding all the other fingers down with the thumb.
Sorry—Close the hand into a soft fist. Rub it softly in a circle on the chest. While doing this, look down and sorrowful.

Say: Jesus told the story of the forgiving father to the people so that they would know:

God forgives us when we do wrong.

Ask: What should we say to God when we treat someone unkindly? *(Sign I'm sorry)*
What should we say to God when we do not share with someone? *(Sign I'm sorry.)*
What do we say to God when we are disobedient to our parents? *(Sign I'm sorry.)*
What do we say to God when we use words that are not very nice? *(Sign I'm sorry.)*
What do we say to God when we take something that does not belong to us? *(Sign I'm sorry.)*

Parable Prayers

Supplies

None

Say: Before we close with our prayer today, I want you to close your eyes and think of this past week. Have there been any times when you have been lost? Did you do something you know you shouldn't have done? Did you mistreat someone on purpose? Then when we pray, during the silent time, I want you to tell God that you are sorry.

Pray: Thank you, God, for the Bible and its stories. They help us know what you are like and how you want us to live. We know we don't always live the way we are supposed to live. *(pause)* **We are so glad that you forgive us when we do wrong. Help us to remember to say** *(Sign I'm sorry)*. **Amen.**

Pat your head and rub your stomach.
Stand on one foot and whistle a tune.
Skip around the circle backwards.
Hold your nose and say the alphabet.
Walk while holding your ankles.
Walk on your knees.
Touch your nose and hop on one foot.
Hop like a bunny around the circle.
Walk like a crocodile.
Walk like an elephant.
Bark like a dog and beg.

Father

Younger Son

Pig Farmer

City Slicker

Pig

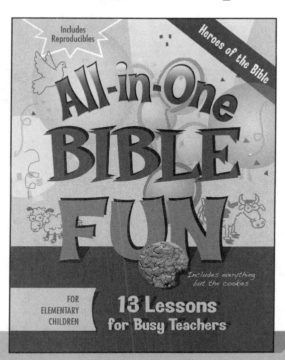

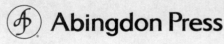

Live B.I.G.

Hear, See, and Live Your Belief in God

Live B.I.G.'s
One Big Room

A Proven Sunday School Program for Mixed-Age Group Children's Ministries

kit includes everything you need for the quarter

- 3 DVDs
- One Music CD
- One Leader Book

For children age 3 through middle school!

Abingdon Press